Tohu-va-vohu ['without Form And Void']

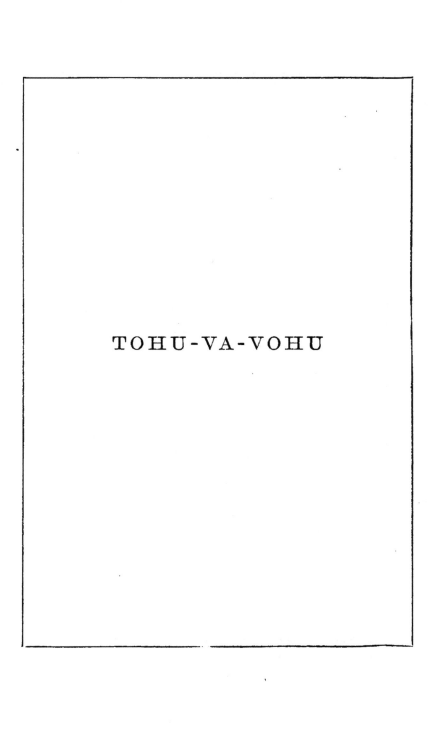

TOHU-VA-VOHU

PRINTED BY
SPOTTISWOODE AND CO., NEW-STREET SQUARE
LONDON

PRINTED BY
SPOTTISWOODE AND CO., NEW-STREET SQUARE
LONDON

VANS, GREEN AND CO.

. YORK: L. PAGE   .

1899

TOHU-VA-VOHU

['WITHOUT FORM AND VOID']

A COLLECTION OF
FRAGMENTARY THOUGHTS AND
CRITICISMS

BY

ALFRED EDERSHEIM, M.A.Oxon., D.D., Ph.D.

SOMETIME GRINFIELD LECTURER ON THE SEPTUAGINT
IN THE UNIVERSITY OF OXFORD

EDITED, WITH A MEMOIR, BY
ELLA EDERSHEIM

WITH A PORTRAIT

LONDON
LONGMANS, GREEN, AND CO.
AND NEW YORK : 15 EAST 16th STREET
1890

PREFACE

In making public the pages of a manuscript book which—with many lapses—was kept by my father during the last seventeen years of his life, it has been thought well to preface them by a short biographical memoir. Material for anything fuller or more satisfactory was not forthcoming, even had it been desirable. Little or no record had been kept of a life singularly full of adventure and interest; and, besides, that the notion of a biography was distasteful to him was well known in his more intimate circle. It has therefore been possible only to touch lightly on the principal events of his career, and it is hoped that the inadequacy and poorness of the result may be leniently regarded. In endeavouring to note some of the most striking features of my father's character, I have tried to avoid panegyric—a restriction rendered more

difficult by the excellence of the subject under treat-
ment. In conclusion, I would record my thanks to
the Rev. Canon Ince, D.D., for the use of papers in
his possession ; to the Rev. Prof. Sanday, D.D., for
his practical help in the preparation of this book ;
and to the Rev. F. A. Overton, for his careful revision
of manuscript and proofs.

E. E.

August 1890.

MEMOIR

ALFRED EDERSHEIM was born of Jewish parents in Vienna on March 7, 1825. His family was of direct high-priestly descent, but did not belong to the narrower and more intolerant sect of the Jews. His father, Marcus Edersheim, was a man of considerable culture and wealth, and occupied a position of some standing in the city, not only as a banker, but as one interested in all intellectual and artistic pursuits. He had originally come from Holland, and had married Fräulein Stéphanie Beifuss, a lady belonging to the well-known Frankfort family of that name. Alfred was the youngest of a family of four, all possessing extraordinary gifts. As a child he was remarkable for his great personal beauty, his peculiar fascination of manner, and the unusual precocity of his intellect. No educational advantage was lacking in his home.

French was acquired even before his mother-tongue, and English was the language commonly used in the family. His father's house was the resort of strangers bringing letters of credit, and in this way many distinguished travellers were entertained.

From earliest years the child had been placed in the hands of a resident tutor, and on attaining the age of ten he entered the Gymnasium. Here he continued to study for the next six years, and it is recorded of him that he was the first Jewish youth in Vienna permitted to carry prizes from that school. At the same time he pursued attendance at the Jewish school in connection with the Synagogue, and here made his first acquaintance with those studies to which he subsequently devoted so much of his time. Full of enthusiasm and ambition, he was already a leader amongst his fellows, and when M. Crémieux, head of the French Bar, visited Vienna, in company with Sir Moses Montefiore, on his return from his noble defence of the Jews against the abominable charges of murder brought against them in connection with their paschal rites, it was young Edersheim who was selected to deliver the French address with which the educated Jewish youth welcomed him. The learned Frenchman was so pleased with the boy's eloquence that he pleaded for him to be allowed to accompany him to Paris and there study for the Bar : but at that time the circumstances of the family were such that no active profession was in contemplation for the younger son.

In 1841, having finished his course at the Gymnasium, Alfred Edersheim entered as a student of philosophy in the University of Vienna. His purpose was, while proceeding ultimately to the degree of M.D., to devote himself in the meantime to literature. For at this date the law regarding the Jews was such that but one son out of each Jewish family was allowed to reside in the city ; and this only if his father enjoyed the privilege of citizenship. The medical profession, however (at that time the only learned profession open to Jews), offered this advantage : that, by being attached to an hospital, temporary residence, and ultimately perhaps citizenship, might be obtained.

Many tales are told of the adventures into which at this time the young student was led by his high spirits. On one occasion he was arrested for mimicry of the sentinels on duty, and was only released when

his father's name had been ascertained. At this
period also he helped to form the first republican
literary club of the University, and his slight, alert
figure, clad in white breeches and black velveteen
coat, with long fair curls lying on his shoulders, was
foremost at every debate and discussion, his ready
eloquence carrying with it the body of opinion of his
fellow-students.

But this happy and congenial life was brought
to an abrupt termination. Scarcely had his first
examination in philosophy been passed with distinction, when the failure of certain Dutch corre-
spondents involved in their ruin his father's bank.
The luxurious *ménage* was hastily suppressed, and
Alfred Edersheim resolved in the future to earn his
own living and make his own way. In spite of the
urgent remonstrances of his family, who would wil-
lingly have shared with him what remained of their
fortune, he set out with only a few dollars in his
pocket for Pesth.

His choice of a university in which to earn his
livelihood and pursue his studies was influenced
by the newly awakened national life of Hungary.
Here more freedom and a larger liberty were to

be found for both Jew and Gentile; here also two
of his former private tutors had settled.

In the University of Pesth, and in spite of his
limited means, young Edersheim soon made for himself a position analogous to that which he had
occupied in Vienna.   His linguistic attainments
easily procured for him pupils, while at the same
time he actively pursued his own studies, and passed
his further examinations.   At this time, also, his first
literary attempt, in the shape of a romantic story,
entitled 'Heinrich,' appeared in the sheets of the
Pannonia, a Pressburg paper, and was accompanied
and followed by other and more ambitious exploits.
These writings drew down on him the warning of
the censorship for their 'dangerous tendency,' and
were probably rashly indicative of that love of entire
liberty which he always retained.

The turning-point in young Edersheim's life—*i.e.*
his conversion to Christianity—was brought about by
those very circumstances which had seemed to be
untoward and disastrous.   Through the introduction
of one of his tutors he had become acquainted with
those Presbyterian Scottish ministers who, under the
protection of the Archduchess Maria Dorothea (by

birth a princess of the house of Würtemberg, and a
Protestant), had come to Pesth, nominally to act as
chaplains to the Scotch colony engaged in construct-
ing the great suspension-bridge across the Danube,
but in reality to found a mission among the Jews.
Into the peculiar and most interesting history of this
mission this is not the place to enter, except in so far
as it affected the destiny of Alfred Edersheim. At its
head stood John Duncan, LL.D., afterwards Professor
of Oriental Languages in the ' New College ' of Edinburgh; a man distinguished not only for his rare genius
and learning, but for the piety and simplicity of his life
and faith. Such a man could not fail to attract and
influence the young student, and an intimacy begun
with him was continued with his delegates, Mr.
Wingate and Mr. Smith, when Dr. Duncan, for
reasons of health, was compelled to retire to Italy.
These two missionaries, on whom the weight of Dr.
Duncan's undertakings now fell, employed young
Edersheim as their teacher in the German language,
and it was in the opportunities thus offered for a further
and thorough study of the New Testament and of
Christianity that the teacher became a learner, and
finally a true and full convert to Christianity.

Writing himself subsequently on this subject, Dr.
Edersheim says : ' The purity and holiness of life of
these men attracted me; their earnestness and convictions aroused me to inquire into the views which
had made them so quite other from those whom I had
hitherto known, and from what I knew myself to be.
Our acquaintance soon ripened into friendship. . . .'
And again : ' I had never seen a New Testament till
I received the first copy from the hands of the
Presbyterian ministers.   I shall never forget the first
impression of " the Sermon on the Mount," nor yet the
surprise, and then deep feeling, by which the reading
of the New Testament was followed.   That which I
had so hated was *not* Christianity; that which I had
not known, and which opened such untold depths, *was*
the teaching of Jesus of Nazareth.   I became a
Christian, and was baptized by the pastor of the
Reformed Church at Pesth.'   That this stage was
followed as well as preceded by long and anxious
thought and struggle, is testified to by a corre-
pondence (in Latin) which ensued between the
newly baptized one and Dr. Duncan, then resident
at Leghorn.

The circumstances which led to the young convert's entering the Presbyterian Ministry are, again, best expressed in his own subsequent words: 'The change in my inner, brought a corresponding change in my outer life. I resolved, instead of devoting myself to literature, to devote myself to the study of theology, and to enter the service of the Church. Of "Church questions" I knew absolutely nothing. They did not as yet arise. I had only learned the doctrines of Christianity from the New Testament, and the only outward church which I really knew (*i.e.* in the sense of being practically acquainted with it) was that of my teachers, the Scottish ministers. . . . Just at that time Dr. Duncan was called to occupy the Chair of Oriental Languages in the newly formed "New College" of Edinburgh; and thither I accompanied him, to study theology in Edinburgh. It was thus naturally and unconsciously (so far as Church questions are concerned) that I became identified with the Presbyterian Church.'

Living under the roof, and working under the personal direction, of Professor Duncan, Alfred Edersheim pursued not only the ordinary branches of theological study, but read exhaustively in dogmatics

—chiefly those of the Reformation period, and then the New England theology. He attended the lectures of Drs. Chalmers, Welsh, and Duncan; and from Edinburgh proceeded to Berlin, where, enrolling himself as a student, he had as professors Hengstenberg, Twesten, Strauss, and the saintly Neander. Having completed his theological *curriculum*, he returned to Scotland and was licensed as preacher, and then ordained presbyter in 1846, the General Assembly in his case specially dispensing with a year on account of his sufficiency in study.

Those were stirring times in Scotland. Only three years before the great disruption in the Church of Scotland had divided the people into opposite camps. Hundreds of parishes were vacant, either so far as the Established or else the Free Church was concerned. Dr. Duncan had cast in his lot with the Free Church, and Alfred Edersheim did the same. The care of no less than four parishes, in the neighbourhood of Kelso, was assigned to him. Days and months of hard work ensued. On Sundays he would preach in three or four different places—barn, smithy, hay-loft, road, hillside serving for church as the exigency of the case might demand. His earnest

ministry was greatly blessed. In six months'
time a regular congregation had gathered round
him, and shortly a pretty church and ' manse ' were
built.

But now a great longing for work among the Jews
came upon him. His task in that part of Scotland
seemed accomplished, and he believed that he recog-
nised God's call elsewhere. Accordingly he resigned
his Scottish post, and travelling through France, Italy,
and Greece, he reached Constantinople, from whence
he proceeded to Roumania. Here he remained for
upwards of a year, teaching and preaching to Jews
and Germans in and about Jassy in connection with
a Scottish mission there established. Here also he
met with Mary Broomfield—one who, like himself,
was deeply interested in mission-work, and a woman
of large and refined intellect. On returning to
Scotland in 1847 he was married to her at the beginning of the following year, and at its close became
assistant minister at Woodside, near Old Aberdeen,
and evening lecturer in the largest church in Aberdeen.
His success as a preacher can scarcely be exaggerated.
Speedily the empty town-church was filled to over-
flowing—pews, aisles, even pulpit-steps were densely

packed, and in four months' time he received the offer
to become minister of the parish of Old Aberdeen.

He himself attributed the returning desire of
study and theological research, not only to the quiet
ensuing upon a more regular and compassable sphere
of duty, but to the associations of learning connected
with Old Aberdeen, the seat of the ancient University.
Perhaps it was also in part due to the inspiration of
home influence that, resuming once more his old
favourite pursuits, he now devoted himself largely to
literature. His studies, ardently pursued far into the
night, soon began to produce appreciable results. His
first book was a translation into English of *Chalybäus'*
' History of Speculative Philosophy,' to which the late
Sir William Hamilton wrote an introduction. Dr.
Chalybäus was *decanus* of the philosophical faculty at
Kiel, and that University acknowledged this work, together with various other contributions which Mr.
Edersheim had made to the better knowledge of
German philosophy in England, by conferring upon
him the degree of Doctor of Philosophy. The transla-
tion of the ' History of Speculative Philosophy ' was
speedily followed by that of *Kurtz's* ' History of the Old
Covenant,' vol. i., together with a condensed abstract of

Kurtz's 'Bible and Astronomy;' then by that of *Kurtz's* 'History of the Christian Church,' vol. i., with additions and emendations; then by that of *Lange's* 'Bible Commentary on St. Matthew' in two volumes. His 'History of the Jewish Nation from the Fall of Jerusalem to the reign of Constantine the Great' was also written at this time, and he was not only attached to the staff of a paper, but contributed regularly to the *Eclectic Review* and the *Athenæum*, as well as to the *North British Review*, the *British and Foreign Review*, and to many other periodicals and magazines.

Hard study and incessant literary work were during this period, indeed, as much a relief as a necessity. A growing comprehension of his own position, of that of the branch of the Church to which he belonged, and of that of the universal Church, raised many and perplexing questions. A study of New Testament criticism and of the Fathers had already, previously to this, led to a complete inward revulsion. It was then, quite at the commencement of this period, as he afterwards said, that his sympathies first turned to the Church of England, although very many years had to pass before he could conscientiously carry these to their full and legitimate conclusion.

In those days party-feeling and bigotry ran so high in Scotland that even to belong to a different section of the Presbyterian Church was scarcely allowed to be compatible with being an earnest Christian. The liberality of Dr. Edersheim's views on some points led to more than one threat of persecution. His sensitive and highly-strung mind felt intensely the want of sympathy, sometimes even suspicion, with which he was regarded. His desires and aspirations became always less in harmony with sectarianism—more catholic.

These and other harassing circumstances, coupled with fifteen years of incessant literary and parochial toil, began to tell upon his health, just as his friends were venturing hopes of his appointment to the professorship of theology in the University of Aberdeen. A heavy cold, caught in the discharge of his duty, settled on his chest, and resulted in a complete breakdown. He was told that his only chance of life lay in immediately and finally quitting Scotland and in retiring to some milder climate. The outlook was very dark, but there was no alternative, and it was decided that he should try the effects of a winter in Torquay.

The winter of 1860–61 accordingly found him once

more a stranger in a strange land, with broken health, with little or no means beyond what lay in his own powers, and with a family dependent on his exertions. His confidence in God as the Father, however, never failed him, and was shortly to be amply justified. At the request of the proprietor of the hotel in which he lodged he consented to take a Sunday afternoon service. The attendance at this on the first day of meeting numbered some half-dozen persons. By the third Sunday the congregation was so large that it had overflowed into the passages and down the stairs. Friends speedily gathered round him. The want of a church for the Scottish residents of, and visitors to, Torquay was specifically felt and formulated; a site was given, funds were collected, and a graceful church, dedicated to St. Andrew, shortly stood in the centre of the pleasure-gardens. Here, once more, Dr. Edersheim's influence as a preacher was widely felt and acknowledged, and here for some years he continued working and giving of his best for the service of God. Here also it was that he lost his first wife, who left him seven daughters and one son, and that he subsequently married Sophia, youngest daughter of the late Admiral John Hancock, C.B.

Under the continual exertion of preaching, and the exhaustion consequent upon it, his health, however, once more gave way. A couple of winters on the Riviera, one spent at Mentone and the other at San Remo, only partially restored him ; the impatience of some of the members of his congregation followed and continually harassed him, and it was thought best that he should retire again from active work to a repose which might be utilised to God's service in literature. In 1872, therefore, he resigned his church at Torquay, and removed to Bournemouth, where he built a villa, which he called *Heniach*, signifying : ' The Lord will give rest.'

During his years of active ministry at Torquay Dr. Edersheim had not enjoyed much leisure for writing. A small collection of hymns, mostly translated from the Latin (' The Jubilee Rhythm of St. Bernard and other Hymns '), had, indeed, appeared, as had also a devotional work entitled, ' The Golden Diary of Heart Converse with Jesus in the Book of Psalms.' He had likewise published a series of lectures on ' Elisha the Prophet: his Life and Times,' and during periods of illness had written several children's stories, of which the best known are :

' True to the End,' ' Robbie and his Mother,' ' Miriam
Rosenbaum,' and 'What is her Name?' Other
magazine work had also engaged him ; but now, at
Bournemouth, he was able for the first time to give
himself heart and soul to those Rabbinic and
Talmudic studies which had always been his delight,
and to face unreservedly and without disturbance
those church questions which for thirty years had
been struggling within him.

The appearance of his book on 'The Temple : Its
Ministry and Services at the Time of Jesus Christ,'
brought him the friendship of the late Canon George
Williams (' Palestine-Williams '), then rector of Ring-
wood, and formerly Senior Fellow of King's College,
Cambridge. This friendship soon ripened into an
intimacy which brought about reciprocal confidence.
Canon Williams was able to enter into the peculiar
development to which Dr. Edersheim's mind had
been subjected. When he had ascertained his views
and convictions, he communicated with the Bishop of
Winchester ; the consequence being, that, in 1875, Dr.
Edersheim was admitted to deacon's, and six months
afterwards to priest's orders, receiving a title from
the late Rev. Zachary Nash as (nominal) curate to the

priory church of Christ Church, Hants. Reference to this change will be found in the *Tohu* on pp. 44 and 45.

In the following year Dr. Edersheim's 'Sketches of Jewish Social Life in the Days of Christ' was published, and he now definitely planned that 'Life and Times of Jesus the Messiah' which was destined to be his *magnum opus*. The idea of this book, and the manner in which he should treat it, had indeed been present with him for very many years. In his student-days the first effects of Strauss's *Leben Jesu* had not yet altogether passed away, and it was then, and while studying that work, that the method which he afterwards pursued occurred to him as the best means of giving a fitting answer to the arguments there employed. The idea, scarcely as yet thoroughly formulated, lay dormant until it received a fresh impetus from the appearance of 'Ecce Homo.' He then drew up the scheme of a book on the basis of his original plan, but this time largely influenced by its reference to the line taken in 'Ecce Homo.' Lack of leisure prevented the accomplishment of this work; and so it came about that it was not till 1876 that Dr. Edersheim found himself in a position to undertake the immense task which he had placed

before him, and this on lines once more modified to
present circumstances. The call to the work, as he
liked to remember, came from without. Through the
introduction of Mr. Reeve, Editor of the *Edinburgh
Review* and late Secretary to the Privy Council,
Dr. Edersheim had become acquainted with Mr. T.
Norton Longman, and it was at the request of this
gentleman that the 'Life and Times of Jesus the
Messiah' was set in hand. In the same year
Dr. Edersheim received the degree of D.D. from the
University of Giessen, and removed to Loders, a
country parish in Dorsetshire, presented to him by
the late Lord Chancellor Cairns. It was during the
seven following years of rural retirement and health-
ful life that his book was written. At the same time
the 'Bible History' (Old Test. Series, now complete in
seven vols.), which he had previously commenced, was
continued, and many other literary engagements were
fulfilled; as, for example, his article on 'Josephus'
for Smith and Wace's 'Dictionary of Christian
Biography,' contributions to the 'Bible Educator,'
the *Edinburgh Review*, and many other minor writings.

In the charge of his poor parishioners, and in

his unremitting care for their temporal as well as spiritual welfare, Dr. Edersheim found the necessary relaxation from his studies, and in the outdoor life and pleasant climate of his parish he regained a large measure of the health and strength which his residence at Bournemouth had already partially restored. In 1880 he was appointed Warburtonian Lecturer at Lincoln's Inn, by the late Archbishop of Canterbury, an office tenable for four years. From this time forward he preached and lectured often in London and elsewhere, and maintained a large and learned correspondence in almost all quarters of the globe.

As his work, and the corresponding intellectual strain, grew, the lack of a congenial and intelligent society became always more conspicuous. His library, the prized collection of a lifetime, was large, and in some departments singularly complete. Yet the want of certain almost unique volumes, and the inconvenience or expense involved in obtaining them, increased in proportion to the continually growing and felt want of discussion and comparison of abstruse or doubtful points with those like-minded with himself. In 1882, Dr. Edersheim resolved to remove to Oxford, an event which synchronized with the completion and appearance of his 'Life and Times of Jesus the Messiah;' and though he always looked back with pleasure on his six years of country life, the step now taken was never regretted. Already, in 1881, the University of Oxford had conferred upon him the degree of M.A. *honoris causa*; in 1883 this was confirmed by decree of Convocation; and in 1884-5 he was appointed Select Preacher to the University. In 1885 his Warburton Lectures were published, under the title of 'Prophecy and History in relation to the Messiah,' and at the same time he was busy with his article on 'Philo' (Smith and Wace's Dictionary of Christian Biography), with further important contributions to the *Edinburgh Review*, *Studia Biblica*, and other periodicals, and with review work (for the *Saturday Review*, the *Guardian*, the *Churchman*, the *Expositor*, the *Church Quarterly*, the *Sunday School Times* (U.S.A.), &c.). In 1886 he was appointed Grinfield Lecturer on the Septuagint in the University of Oxford, an office to which in 1888 he was re-elected. In Oxford also he completed his 'Bible History,' and in 1886 he undertook his 'Commentary on Ecclesiasticus,' for the 'Speaker's Commentary on the Apocrypha,' a work in which he was assisted by Prof. Margoliouth. The

Commentary, a monument of careful and scholarly labour, occupied the greater part of two years, and was a severe strain on his energies. The extent of the work involved was far larger than he had foreseen, and was more specially trying in that he was, at this time, busy collecting materials for, and anxious to get to the writing of, a second large book, a companion to his 'Life and Times.' This was to have been the 'Life and Writings of St. Paul,' and was definitely undertaken in 1887, at the request once more of Mr. Norton Longman, with whom, since his first introduction in 1876, Dr. Edersheim had been on terms of the warmest friendship.

Opportunity for beginning this fresh work was lacking until 1888, when its first chapters were written with the keenest delight and the most eager anticipation. That delicacy of health, however, to which he was subject, and against which for so many years he had successfully striven, once more over-mastered him. A slight cold, which immediately settled on the chest, gave the preliminary warning of what was to follow. By the advice of his friend and medical adviser, Dr. Nankivell (of Bournemouth), it was decided once again to try the effects of a winter on the Riviera, together with complete rest and quiet. Mentone—where he had spent the winter of 1869–70—was chosen, as being a place to which his memory always returned in an enthusiasm of pleasure. Among its olive-groves and under its blue sky he had been able to realise those aspects of the Holy Land which he had afterwards so intimately described in the 'Life and Times.' Here for five short months life and the enjoyment of life returned to him. He speedily lost the overwhelming languor and lassitude which had been on him, and entered with his usual zest into all matters of daily interest. Already he had planned a return-journey home by the northern towns of Italy and its lakes, when suddenly, and without any premonitory symptom—

'God's finger touched him and he slept.'

On a spur of the beautiful hill-side cemetery of Mentone he lies, looking straight towards Jerusalem, the city whose people he loved and tried to serve, and in whose spiritual counterpart he now beholds his King in all His beauty; and, having awaked up after His likeness, is satisfied with it.

In giving the foregoing sketch of the outward life and circumstances of Dr. Edersheim, it has not been possible sufficiently to indicate those mental characteristics and peculiarities which made his a nature difficult to understand—more especially by those of a wholly differing nationality and training—but, when once grasped, possessing a charm which was found to amount to a positive fascination. His mind was at first baffling; his qualities seemed to lead to contradictory, or at least unexpected, results. Thus the gentleness of his disposition would not betray him into yieldingness, and his large tolerance of, and sympathy for, widely-differing opinions, never resulted in the loss of his own convictions, or of what he had once grasped as the truth. A further illustration of this was his position as a Churchman. He was at once too liberal-minded and too critically disposed to identify himself with any one party. Having certain sympathies with each, he adhered closely to none, but preferred to class himself simply as a loyal son of the Church. With consistency in its more rigid forms he had little or no sympathy (as may be seen by a reference to pp. 115–7 of the *Tohu*): he was convinced of the necessity of a development, an evolution, in minds possessing the fundamental principles of life and growth. His own development had been so gradual that but shortly before the end he expressed its incompleteness and further possibilities. It will be necessary to hold this principle of his clearly in view for a proper understanding of the varying, and sometimes seemingly contradictory, statements contained in the *Tohu*. Many of its thoughts, also, are only properly to be understood when the circumstances under which they were written are taken into consideration. Thus on page 10 the remark on 'trees of righteousness' was evidently suggested by the fashion of planting a tree to commemorate the building of a house—as was done at Bournemouth at the time when he made this entry, and was building his own villa. And a good deal of what is referred to as 'modern theology' (*e.g.* on pp. 14, 19, 24, 46) was suggested by the great wave of Revivalism which accompanied and followed Messrs. Moody and Sankey's visit to this country, and which was largely felt at Bournemouth. For of a familiar meddling with holy things he was alone intolerant, often saying that people 'tramped in with seven-and-sixpenny boots where angels feared to enter.'

The *Tohu*, begun about the year 1872, and bearing a characteristic dedication to his wife, may, indeed, be described as in great measure a diary—unfortunately too spasmodically kept—recording the inward impressions prominent at the moment, and which in turn were the product not only of outward circumstances, but of his own mental and spiritual development. In it also may be found the gist of his thinking on certain difficult subjects, here tersely noted down, and often to be found more fully developed in the writings which had first raised the train of thought (comp. *e.g.* *Tohu*, pp. 74 and 75, and ' The Life and Times,' vol. ii., pp. 471-8). Its last entry, made March 16, 1889, will be found unfinished. This, perhaps, is the only known instance of an uncompleted sentence from his pen : a type of the day on which it was written, and which was destined to be left unfinished here, and of that life so suddenly and abruptly cut short.

With a mind and habit of thinking essentially scholarly, and with a sensitiveness of disposition which made him keenly alive to much that might pass unnoticed by many of robuster sort, Dr. Edersheim retained a vast fund of humour (often resulting in a most comical mimicry), and an intense interest in all the questions of life—political, scientific, domestic. It was this combination of traits which made him so essentially ' human.' As was well said of him in one of the notices which appeared in the spring of last year, ' the man was more than his books '—and this, perhaps, was only fully realised by those who were most intimately connected with him. His conversation was of a peculiarly brilliant order, sparkling with epigram and illustration, and with what, for lack of a better term, may perhaps be described as metaphorical analogies. His knack of placing himself on the same standing with even the most trivial of those who had intercourse with him; his unfailing patience with the endless and, as it often seemed, wanton demands of his questioners; his chivalric courteousness to those below him in station; his wise friendship, in the exercise of which he would never spare himself; his tenderness and love for children and for animals—all these qualities, combined with his great acquirements, and lightened and vivified by his penetration and humour, made him that which he was, and was worthy to be called : the model of a Christian scholar and gentleman.

TOHU-VA-VOHU

———◦•◦———

IT is a beautifully significant idea, that the Jews, after fulfilling any commandment or ordinance of the Law, specially thank God for having given it—to show that the Law is not a burden, but a privilege. This is the *formula*: 'Who hast sanctified us by Thy commandments and enjoined us [e.g. " to remove the leaven "].'

There is infinite comfort and hope even in the fact of being God's creature—the work of His Hand.

' Jehovah reigneth '—these two words contain both the Law and the Gospel.

It is a beautiful saying of Rabbi Jochanan, that wherever in Scripture you find the greatness and

B

majesty of God, you also find at the same time His condescension. So in the Law, then in the Prophets, and again in the Hagiographa.

I imagine there is nowhere in Nature either a gap or a sudden transition, but always intermediate and connecting links. Thus between lifelessness and life (stones and plants), between plants and animals, and again between instinct and reason (animals and men), in that highest class of instinct which almost simulates reason. Generally, *language* is regarded as the highest attribute of man; I regard it as the lowest. It must be either the product of a kind of higher instinct— which is unreasoning reason—or else of inspiration (strange that these two, the highest and the lowest in the scale, should meet!), so deeply significant is it. For I cannot believe that nations had reasoned it all out, and then put it down in their languages—all this deep philosophy of their grammars, of the derivation of their words, and even of their idioms. Take such a simple instance of the latter as this: In England, where we are least reasoning, we say: ' It is cold,' meaning, the air is cold, which is nonsense—since cold and heat are not real attributes, but mark our subjective feelings. In French we advance to: ' *Il fait froid,*' which means, It produces cold; while in German we have it: '*Es thut kalt,*' It affects one cold, which is the true thing.

There are even good people who suffer from religious or, still worse, from theological *dyspepsia.* Beware of spiritual biliousness. Perhaps it is best cured homœopathically—i.e. *similia similibus.* Put two of these people together—that is, if they are both genuine.

I am afraid I am not becoming more—what they call—orthodox; but I hope I am becoming more Christian. Formerly I used to find it much easier to be orthodox than now. I suppose I was working with thinner ropes. But now these two ropes—free grace and human responsibility—have grown so very large in my hands, that I am not strong enough to tie them together.

If I did not believe in the perseverance of saints, I could no longer believe in the Saviour Himself. For is it not so that at our conversion we put ourselves with perfect confidence into the hands of Christ, to be saved by Him?—and salvation would scarce be worth having

if, after so giving up ourselves unto Him, He could in
the end leave us. It were such breach of plighted
troth as one dares not contemplate in connection with
God.   ' Oh, but,' you say, ' is not that to encourage
the false confidence of hypocrites ? '   I answer :
' Friend, religion was never made for the hypocrites,
but only for the genuine ; it contains no provisions
against possible abuses or fraud. The *law* is made
" for the lawless and disobedient," not the Gospel,
which is " the children's " provision. And lastly, " he
that is filthy, let him be filthy still."   Scripture never
heeds these things : it goes on in its majestic grandeur
and stately triumph, never heeding the little yelping
curs that come out of every by-lane to snarl and
bark.'

A gentleman is not a ponderable quantity,
weighing so many pounds sterling ; nor does it repre-
sent so much lamp-black, in the shape of acquirements
(or rather accretions, say deposits, in the shape of
unburnt carbonic) ; nor yet so much polish––whether
of the furniture or the patent-leather kind ; but a man
who is gentle, and being gentle is yet a man.   The old
heathen
    Scilicet ingenuas didicisse fideliter artes
    Emollit mores, nec sinit esse feros

was a great deal better than our modern ideas, but fell far short of the Christian gentleman.

People should be very careful about urging on others to leave a Church. I am sure I would rather, so long as I could, keep even a bad tooth than—not to speak of the pain of the pulling—have an empty gum or a false tooth. The Dissenters very liberally offer to present to us a set of new teeth, *gratis*, free for nothing, if we will only part with the old. These teeth, we are told, have many advantages: you do not require to clean them; they never cause an ache; you can take them out and in at will; and you can improve on their appearance and substance. Nevertheless, I prefer keeping my old case, though many of them are far gone!

This, however, is not to say that it may not under any circumstances be duty to leave a Church.

People who are very particular about secondary matters are never very earnest about primary. The greatest prude is not generally the most modest woman; I distrust the generalship of the soldier who is a martinet, and I doubt the reality of those theologians who are so rabid about smaller points. As for myself, I could not get up even a show of enthusiasm on such topics.

For a long time I was a negative Presbyterian— that is, I remained such because I did not see anything absolutely perfect. I wished to have the life of Brethrenism, the form of Episcopacy, and the constitutional rights and liberties [1] of Presbyterianism.

When a man objects to another being called *Reverend*, the presumption is, he would like to be called so himself.[2] There is as much error in making the absence of trifles vital as in insisting on their presence.

I shrink from Dissent. It is mainly a negative thing. If you were to define it, it would be chiefly in negatives: what it is *not*; but not what it *is*. We want not so much the *destructive* as the *constructive* in religion.

[1] A later note adds : ' These exist only in theory,' with a few other remarks. There is also the following addition to the sentence: ' Thank God, I am beyond this, and within the historical Church.'

[2] The reference here is to certain scruples of the ' Plymouth Brethren ' and ' Open Brethren,' with whom, at this period, the writer was a good deal thrown in contact.

For a good many religious statements and preachers' inferences there is no other Scripture reference than to Eph. xii. 95 !

Bengel is right. These are the four stages :

Sine timore et sine amore ;
Cum timore et sine amore ;
Cum timore et cum amore ;
Sine timore et cum amore.

There are four wonderful things about Israel : their election, their rejection, their unbelief, and their ingathering.

Israel's first sin was in asking, their last in rejecting, a king.

I like a republic, but I detest a democracy.

The difference between Judaism and Christianity is as great as between Judaism and early heathenism. Hence gradual progress was necessary, and the onward development and changes which we notice, for example, in the Maccabean period as compared with the earlier, could not have been awanting, as the advance in the Kingdom of God is never *per saltum.*

It must have been an immense reformation which David brought about, when we compare the state of semi-heathenism under Saul with such a hymnology as that introduced by David. No wonder that, despite all his failings, he was called ' a man after God's own heart.'

Saul, like most men risen from the dregs, was intensely jealous—which in such cases means self-conscious.

There are two wonderful things by which the Bible shows its Divine knowledge of the human heart and the world's need : it lifts up to a moral level those who are low, and it leads to voluntary self-abasement those who are high.

Currenti occurrit is a principle which holds good of all God's dealings in grace, whether at our conversion or afterwards in our Christian progress.

Love is not self-conscious. Why should our love to God be always self-inspective ?

There are two ways of looking upon the Cross: from above downwards, and from below upwards. As God sees it, it is all finished and accepted ; as we see it, it is a mode of salvation to which we must struggle upwards. But God would not have it so. He says : ' Stand fast in the liberty wherewith Christ has made you free.'

Our Churchism is mostly like withered leaves—showing where life *has been*.

There are two facts which are never past: the Crucifixion and the Resurrection of Christ.

In Scotland they mostly learn the New Testament through the Old ; in England, the Old Testament through the New.

There is a great difference between waiting on Providence, and being a ' hanger-on ' upon Providence. The distinction is very much the same as between two men, one of whom is in regular service to a master, while the other is looking out for odd jobs that may come in.

' Trees of righteousness : the planting of the Lord.'
When the Lord visits man, He plants His ' memorial-
trees ' everywhere. These are His Saints.

Man's forgiveness is *quantitative* (' how often shall
my brother sin against me ? '). God's forgiveness is
qualitative. Man forgives *sins* ; God forgives *sin*.

God's forgiveness both cleans and cleanses ; man's
can do neither.

God reckons with us when He sets before us
the demands of the Law : This do and thou shalt live !
But He does not reckon with us when He sets before
us the provision of the Gospel. He *has* reckoned with
Christ.

To the grand Humanitarianism and Utilitarianism
that looks down upon evangelical doctrine with the
question : ' Why all this waste ? ' we reply : ' Friends,
your prototype is Judas Iscariot, from whom you have
learned the question. But I greatly doubt whether,
if they handed you over the bag, you would do more
good to the poor than he did when he carried it. The
truth is : " He was a thief," that is, he wanted it all for

himself; and what good have *you* ever done in the world ?'

It is the Form of the transfigured Christ which, like the pillar of fire at night during Israel's journey through the wilderness, moves on before us and so lights up the valley of the shadow of death. We see it enter the tunnel, as it were, and mark the track of light before us. And then it comes out the other side, and climbs the bright bank on which heaven has lavished the beauty of an eternal spring.

All I really know of God—all I want to know of God—is *in Christ*. *My* God is only God in Christ: I know no other, and I do not want to know any other than as there revealed.

It is a common mistake to speak of Scripture-biographies. Scripture does not give us any biography: it writes not any man's life; it writes the history of God's purposes and dealings, and man comes in so far as he is affected by them or reflects them. Scripture traces the track of light in its progress; and objects come in view as the light necessarily falls on them. Hence the immense gaps

in the lives of even such men as Abraham, Moses,
St. John and St. Paul, where sometimes thirty or
forty years are scarcely filled by one sentence.

. Theologians have what seems to me a very
erroneous manner of speaking about the Law, which
must have come to them from the system known as
the 'Federal Theology.' We are told that all men
are under the Law, by which is meant the Law of
Moses. On inquiring more particulars, you are then
told that only that portion of it is meant which is
called the Moral Law, and is contained in the Ten
Commandments. But, granting the distinction for
the sake of argument, the statement is not true. The
nations could not be under a Law of which they were
ignorant, and which was destined for Israel alone.
Nor does St. Paul in Rom. i. and ii., or in any other
passage, ever hint such a relationship. Light is
thrown on the subject by our Lord's summary of the
Law as perfect love to God, and love to our neighbour
equal to that for ourselves. Under this law, whether
graven on the conscience or more clearly spoken in
the 'ten words,' *all* men are—and the breach of this
law must carry death : indeed, it *is* death. The
Gentiles are only under the Law of Moses in so far as
it is the fullest expression of the Law of Nature.

Even Exodus xx. 2 shows that the Ten Commandments were intended for Israel (and not for the Gentiles). For the ground on which they are founded is the fact of Israel's deliverance by Jehovah.

Even a mistaken answer to a difficulty is in some sort an answer to it. It shows *there is* a way out of it, though I may not have found the right way as yet. Only that to which no rational answer at all can be offered is a real difficulty.

Christ and other masters! But by His side there are no other masters. Not to speak of the heathen, what a contrast between the concentrated essence of Jewish wisdom and piety and the words of Christ. Suppose you even proved that much in His sayings found a counterpart in Rabbinical authorities—what then? In the one case you have a little gold with much dross; in the other, pure gold without any dross. Whence the difference?

Christ in His age, in His country, among His people, in the midst of Rabbinism, is a unique Person —One, as God is One; One, isolated and apart—a Divine Master among human teachers and learners.

Christ says : ' I am the door.' If the door is so
glorious, what must be the building into which it
opens !

With reverence be it said : Our modern theology
has almost lost sight of the Father. Our thoughts
and our prayers are almost exclusively directed to the
Second Person of the Godhead. Yet it is to the
Father we are to come through the Son and by the
Holy Spirit ; and it was the object of the Son to reveal
the Father, through the Holy Spirit given unto us.

When I try to think about Divine things I feel as
a man would, who, if he had the power of flying,
attempted to do so in a room. I immediately knock
my head against the ceiling, and come bumping down
on the floor.

Remember : a *reply* is not necessarily an *answer*.
You may silence a man, and yet he may quite
rationally remain unconvinced. For to demolish the
argument of another is quite a long way off from
proving your own position. If you have pulled down
my house, you have not yet built your own in its

place. I think it is Kant who somewhere remarks that the *reductio ad absurdum* is about the most unsatisfactory mode of argumentation : that is, as I understand it, a negative does not prove a positive. I may be a fool for saying that it is Monday, but that does not yet prove that it is Tuesday.

It is a common mistake to suppose that the mercy-seat over the ark was sprinkled with blood. On the Day of Atonement the blood was sprinkled *towards* the mercy-seat and the ark (that is, upwards and downwards), but never *on* the mercy-seat. The mercy-seat itself was an emblem of Christ ; and the blood-sprinkling towards the ark, of the restoration alike of the covenant (sprinkling down towards the ark) and of covenant-mercy (sprinkling up towards the mercy-seat) ; or, of the renewal of the covenant and of covenant-mercy by the same means by which they had at first been established, viz. sacrificial blood.

Christianity is a constant negation. Its teaching is a negation of what naturally occurs to the mind ; its practice a negation of what naturally presents itself to the imagination and the heart.

Practical Christianity is a constant saying : ' No ! no ! no ! ' to all around—the world, the flesh, the devil—and, not unfrequently, to the so-called Church too.

Every party or division in the Church was in its origin the representative of some vital truth, at the time overlooked or denied, and only became a *sect* when the truth it had embodied either lost its vitality, or else after the real object of the party had been attained, and the truth which it originally carried forth made its way everywhere.

I hate those fussy ' unsworn brokers ' of religion who are always trying ' to do business.' If *you* will give up a little, and *he* will give up a little, you will meet ! If *you* don't hold by this doctrine so tightly, and *he* by that opposition ; *you* concede that God does not hear men about the weather, and *he* that God can influence the will in answer to prayer—well, and what then ? You self-important little conceit of a being ! You may get the two to shake hands over it and sip weak tea ; but you can never get truth and error to meet together.

Somehow the tempter must have knowledge of our thoughts, since his temptations are so adapted to them. I do not believe he can search our minds and hearts; but I suppose he can read our actual thinking, which is printed mind, as it were, just as we read the pages of a book.

Of all reasoning in theology, the inferential is the most unsatisfactory. Your logic may be irreproachable, and yet your conclusion false. For possibly it may turn out that there was something in the Divine *major* or *minor* of which you on earth were ignorant.

An inference is what *you* carry into a thing. But what if I refuse to *admit* it?

When you charge me with an inference, you say in substance: If I were in your place I would think or do so-and-so! But then you are *not* in my place, and I refuse to put myself into yours.

All unreality, all ultraism, and all uncharity in religion are derived from *inferences*. You first sup-

c

pose a thing to be, and then straightway deal with it as a fact.

There is very little in the New Testament that bears on what we call our ' Church principles.' And yet I do not know any Church that does not differ, in fewer or more points, each from the little which the New Testament says on such matters.

Considering the manner in which most people reason, one is thankful even to find a person who can point out correctly the difficulties that are in the way. Such an one will *show* you the way, if he cannot *clear* it. For if I want to go to a place, there is a great deal in having the way tracked out, even though it is not made.

To become, and not always *to get*—such should be my motto in prayer. May not the opposite explain much of the poverty in prayer ?

Neither is it sanctification that causes justification, nor yet justification that causes sanctification. The cause of both alike is our new relationship towards God through and in Christ. Hence the

Apostle preached, 'repentance towards God, and faith towards our Lord Jesus Christ.'

A strange confusion and legalism some nowadays would call such preaching !

I cannot find terms too strong to express my abhorrence of the conceit, self-righteousness, narrow-mindedness, folly, and perversion of Christianity of some modern sectaries. Theologically speaking, they are dangerous lunatics, who, in their own opinion, are too good for this world. And if it were left to them, what a mess they would make of it !

'Citizens of another world,' say they, and therefore we must not take part in anything connected with the State or society. As if our Lord had not given His sanction to civil society when, in paying the tribute, He pointed to the image and superscription on the coin ; and St. Paul, when he insisted on his rights as a Roman citizen, and afterwards appealed unto Cæsar ! Would it be believed that they think the standpoint of our Lord and of St. Paul in so doing was below theirs ? Not: *O sancta simplicitas* ; but: O PROFANA *simplicitas !*

Some of these sectaries may be excellent wine— but, ah me ! it is dreadfully corked !

I can imagine few more severe trials of patience than to have to *reason* with a regular sectary. The Italian proverb has it : 'You may see heaven even through a very small hole.' But that is a very different thing from seeing it *only* in that way !

In all healthy religion, enjoyment and service should advance *pari passu*—both proceeding from the same cause : solid, internal growth.

I can say a great many things in favour of the Lord Jesus Christ—of His Power, Grace, and Love. But the greatest I can say of them is : that He has received *me*. Thus the faith of the poorest sinner brings the greatest glory to Christ.

Christianity needs neither apologetics nor apologies. It is not intended for ' the wise ' nor ' the prudent,' but for ' babes.'

The chief use of apologetics is to answer a fool according to his folly ; that is, to silence him.

There are people who express themselves with such elaborate distinctness as to become at last indistinct, repeating and re-repeating till they succeed in bamboozling themselves and every other person.

Let those who so confidently meddle with things too high for them, remember that people should not stamp in with heavy club-nailed boots upon velvet pile carpets.

The heart of man is a many-stringed harp. One Hand alone can sweep all its cords, and that is the Hand which was nailed to the Cross.

Abraham represents the life of faith; Isaac of sonship; Jacob of service; Joseph of rule.

Our need and our faith are two hands to draw us to Christ.

Everything that came before Christ looked to Christ; everything that came after Christ followed from Christ.

There is no depth so deep but the everlasting Arms are underneath.

Our friends, the Plymouth Brethren, feel that in the Holy Scriptures they have got into a magnificent forest, and they straightway set themselves most busily to cut it up into toothpicks.

It is not the sinner, but the sinning, who should tremble.

Justification is the credit side, Sanctification the debit side, of the Christian life.

The breastplate of the high priest indicated not, as generally supposed, his intercession for the people, but his representation of Israel.

Thank God for what He reveals, and thank God for what He conceals. The faith which follows God into the light is supplemented and completed by that which follows Him in the dark.

I do not see any reason to deny the intercession of the saints in heaven, either for those whom they loved on earth, or for the progress of the kingdom of God. This does not by any means imply our invocation of their intercession, which could only be warrantable if they were omniscient or omnipresent; while their spontaneous intercession is due to their continuous interest and affection towards what had engaged them on earth.

Remember in religion and in life: For fungus-growths it needs no more than a dark, damp place!

It is necessary not only to be entirely truthful, but to speak out the truth, so far as we are capable of perceiving it. To speak it in love is a Christian grace. Only remember: the truth—not *my* truth nor *thine,* but *the* truth catholic, that is, *semper, ubique, ab omnibus* avowed as the truth.

When after a weary day and a long evening of mutual humbugging, people take off their false ringlets and take out their false teeth, smooth themselves and undo their ruffles, and stand out in their native limpness just before going to bed—physically, mentally, and morally, how mean and jaded they must look in the glass, and how miserable they must feel!

There are few things I dread more in religion than arguments in its favour. They are mostly wretched

exhibitions of our own weakness, not proofs of its
strength.   The best argument for religion is to show
it.   No one can deny its reality then.   Prove religion
by your lives rather than by your words.

Let us beware of impertinent familiarity in religion,
such as some make their so-called assurance.   It is
the old story of the *parvenu*, who tries to push himself
into the closeness of intimate converse by vulgar, rude
familiarity.   He that is ' to the manner born,' the real
child, has and needs none of that obtrusive familiarity.
God should be approached with reverence and holy
awe—and most of all by His own children, who know
Him best.

Most people are wretchedly miserable, though they
will not allow themselves to know it.   It is a weary
thing to be always play-acting—sometimes for bread,
and sometimes for even less than that—while sorrow
wrings our heart.

It may sound strange, but when we come to the
innermost springs of our lives, there should be no
' because ' in what makes them flow.   A flower bursts
into bloom for no other ' because ' than that it *is* a

living flower. Similarly, a man says, does, lives that which is right, true, or good, for no 'because' connected either with this world or the next, but simply for that he is renewed in the image of Christ. It is this constant incursion of a 'because' which makes our lives and our religion so much of a play-acting : the 'because' has put a *rôle* upon us which is not our real, spontaneous self.

Assuredly, if a 'because' is the father who begets my moral acting, then my actions are, so far as my innermost being is concerned, bastards, not sons.

Is that the reason why faith must lie at the root of all spiritual life ? For faith is the immediate reception of the higher life, whereas the 'because,' with its strongest motive impelling or forcing us to will and to do, is in its nature of the character of Law.

Even failure becomes precious when the effort has been my own, and not dragged after it by a 'because.'

A *raison d'être* does not really mean a reason for being, but an object in being : it refers to the future, not to the past. The only reason for our being is

God—as for our *raison d'être*, it begins after that. It is given us of God, in order to work out the true *être*. We live in order to live. But how few know what *être* means! The humblest life and work may be *être*, if it is really spiritual and spiritually real.

That which has no object in being has also no longer any reason for being. Remember this in your life and religion.

Repent quickly, or else I will remove thy candlestick, saith Christ.

The commonest and yet most dreadful of sins is untruthfulness. It comprises a breach of all the Ten Commandments; it makes a man a villain, a coward, and a sneak all together; it lowers one's estimate of oneself, and it cuts off every bud of possible growth or development. Yet how many of us have been untruthful from hunger pangs? I feel and can have hope for such; not so for other forms of it.

Who am I that condemn another? The Master bears with him! It is the old story of the much forgiven, and his harshness towards him who owes the few pence.

Jacobi is not far wrong in ascribing our anthropomorphisms in thinking of God to the theomorphism of our nature.

There is a vast difference between self-sacrifice and suicide. In regard to all scriptural sacrifices the necessary pre-requisites are : that the kind, the place, and the manner of sacrifice shall be expressly ordered of God. Is it so in all that we call self-sacrifice ? If not, it seems to come under the genus suicide rather than sacrifice.

What we call Providence is the presence of God in His creation, and His administration of its laws in accordance with the moral and gracious purposes of His government. In one sense there is no special Providence ; in another all Providence is special. What makes a Providence special is not any alteration of God's laws, nor yet of His administration of them, but of our bearing towards them. It becomes special from our special relationship towards them. The Hand of God does not alter the law of nature ; but it may alter my relationship in reference to it. The stone that falls will crush ; but I may be pushed out of the way, or it may be diverted before reaching me. In short: in reference to forces, God deals as a Force; in reference to persons, as a Person.

Passion and weakness are the sharps and flats in the melody of our souls. It depends on the key of a tune whether the same tones shall be sharps or flats; and, after all, they are perhaps only the semitones of our poor fallen nature.

If I were an infidel—which God forbid—I would hide myself and my discoveries from sight of men. It seems to me the strangest philanthropy to insist upon making men unspeakably miserable by taking from them every hope of the future, and worse than brutes by depriving them of every ground and motive for truth, morality or devotion.

Why *anything*, if all is matter, and there is neither God nor immortality? Assuredly, no inference can be more logical from the premises than this: 'Let us eat and drink, for to-morrow we die.'

I am devoutly thankful to God for every evidence in favour of Christianity. Each is a joyous discovery.

Believe—or rather experience—that He saith unto thee : ' Thy sins are forgiven thee,' and thou *must* love Him who saith it. And loving Him, thou canst sin no more. Sin will be quite another thing to thee than before; not only its power, but its character quite different. It is no longer a mortal disease ; only the consequences of that which had been in thee before.

In the world of thought and of life, neutrality is a moral impossibility ; it is moral death. Taken in one signification of the term, neuter is *not either,* nor yet both. Then what is it ? It is beyond my horizon, out of my sphere, a mere existence, but an existence without the attributes of existence, a substantive without adjectives, which is logically unthinkable and morally non-existent. Or take its other meaning : *neuter,* neither masculine nor feminine, not even that *lusus naturæ,* hermaphrodite. Then what is it ? A thing, an *it,* not even a force, but a dead weight ! So true is it that this world of ours is dead without moral impulses.

Hitzig beautifully compares the Jewish people to the pearl oyster, which in dying gives its treasure to the world.

I am spiritually almost as much indebted to
Providence as to grace.   Therefore, whoever else may
find himself unable so to do, I, at least, can pray
from the bottom of my heart: 'Lead us not into
temptation!'

Much that passes for evangelical teaching is like
brushing a napless coat.   You may make it shiny,
but you only show the more clearly that there is no
wool on the cloth.

The world is full of clever people—till it is almost
a relief to find a genuine fool.   But the worst thing
that can happen is when one of these clever people
takes to writing about religion.

> Odi profanum vulgus et arceo.
> Favete linguis!

They who would write a Life of Christ aright must
themselves also begin (in heart and soul) as the
Gospels begin—with the angels' song, the worship of
the shepherds, and the gifts of the Magi.   Or if they
would preach to us from it they must begin like John
with this: 'Behold the Lamb of God, which taketh
away the sin of the world.'   If otherwise, they have

not gone to the right door, and will never get into the house.

Yet, to give even the devil his due—as our modern honest debtors of that great creditor say—these modern Lives of the Lord Jesus have, not done good, but served an important purpose, though all unconsciously to themselves.

It is a humbling fact, that no sooner dies a giant than the worms immediately set to work : when he ceases to reign, they begin to feast. And what a number of them, and how busy ! Every great event in history, every great person, is such a giant—and immediately afterwards come the worms. So it was when Christianity first appeared on earth—immediately afterwards the heresies ; when the Reformers passed away, immediately after them the sectaries. Worms innumerable, with all sorts of scientific names. Thank God, the deluge of infidelity has swept them away into naturalists' collections, where you see them only labelled.

Then came back the great question of questions— the immense skeleton lay there : Can it live again ? What think ye of Christ ? And because that is *the* question to which these (bio)graphies of the great

Life has narrowed all our controversies, therefore I
bless God for every one of them, even for the very
worst.

Men and brethren, sophists, sycophants, rational-
ists, naturalists, materialists, and clever people all :
what can be the use of fighting about adjectives ?
Let us come to the substantive ! What is the purpose of quarrelling and breaking each other's heads ?
for wooden skulls will break, or at least be indented.
If there is no such thing as a rose, why will you quarrel
about its being either red or white, great or small,
prickly or smooth ? What is the good of attacking
inspiration, or the fall, or miracles, or this or that
book in the Bible, if Jesus of Nazareth is not the
Christ, the Son of the Living God ? But if He is—do
you think it still worth while to fight about the other
things ; *can* you do so ? One miracle or revelation is
enough for me—and this one contains all the others.
So *ad rem.* Our French masters have it : *Dis-moi
qui tu hans et je te dirai qui tu es.* I would rather
reverse it, not being a phenomenal man : *Dis-moi
qui tu es et je te dirai qui tu hans.* So we have
got from the worms to the life-students : from the
exegetes, the dogmatists, the apologetes, the historians

—to the biographers. How will they study that life? Anatomically, physiologically, pathologically? How will they explain the origin of that life? Chemically, dynamically, biologically or molecularly?

We have got Strauss: a German. There are floating ideas, and then men set to realise them. And that is the origin of Christianity. Similarly this is the origin of the world: there are a number of insects flying about, and men are straightway created on purpose to catch them—and that is all! *Plaudite*!

People like Strauss's Christ and Apostles never lived—never existed save in the inner consciousness of a theorist.

Next comes Renan. Now it is not mysticism, but all *esprit*. An enthusiast and self-deceiver, who from the first walks steadily up to the Cross! Assuredly, Jesus never had any illusions—and yet He is an enthusiast!

The *Ecce Homo* gives us the Christ of polite, well-bred society, the Messiah of English common-sense and order. A wretched commonplace specimen of religious respectability, dressed in a social frock-coat, and fit for any luncheon party. What a caricature! Yet this is the ideal of such intelligences as Mr. ——'s, the high-point of wide-talked mediocrity.

——'s *Life of Christ* reminds me of an official guide through a gallery. He knows everything, tells you everything, and in wonderful language—but has no judgment or appreciation of his own, and is an awful bore.

Of all things, the most unlike Christ are His times.

I have found it most difficult of all simply to submit to God, and not to try to direct my own destinies. Yet this is the grand lesson of Jacob's life.

Instead of 'honest doubters' we might frequently write 'honest debtors.' There is no need to name *him* of whom they have borrowed their stock-in-trade.

There are many more A-nomians than Antinomians, both in the Church and in the world.

With God the subjective and the objective—what He thinks and wills and what He is—are absolutely one; with us they are not only distinct but opposite poles. This may give us some glimpse how the mystery of predestination may be solved, and also explain why *we* can never hope to understand it.

Truth and experience must become one in healthy Christian life. Every experience must spring from truth, and every truth must become experience. I do not believe in any truth which is incapable of becoming experience. In this respect also: ' With the heart it is believed unto righteousness.' The objective must become subjective, part of my inner being, or it exists not for me any more than do outward objects which are not perceived by the senses.

Spiritual life has its double beat of the heart: receiving all from God, and bringing all to God, as it is written: ' All my springs are in Thee.'

This verse, ' All my springs are in Thee,' contains the mystery of perfect wisdom, perfect righteousness, perfect sanctification, and perfect redemption.

The Korahite Psalms differ specially in this from the Asaphite, that the former treat chiefly of the Kingdom, the latter of the King.

This is the correct rendering of 1 St. Pet. iii. 21 : 'Which (water) also, as the antitype, now saves us, even baptism—not the putting away of the filth of the flesh, but the inquiry (the searching) after a good conscience towards God, through the resurrection of Christ.'

Note :

(1) Baptism is the search after a good conscience towards God, the renewed heart seeking after holiness ; it is a seeking (as it were) for admission into a state of grace, the renouncing of the world, the devil, and the flesh, and as such it saves us.

(2) Not the act of baptizing or being baptized, but *baptism* saves us.

(3) It does so antitypically, as answering or corresponding to the type of the Noachic flood that buried the old world that a new one might spring in its stead.

As when the old world lay submerged in water, the dove carrying the one olive-branch to Noah in the

Ark indicated the return of life, which anon would burst forth in a new world, clothed in the green of a fresh spring, so when our Blessed Lord was baptized, and the Holy Ghost in the form of a dove hovered above Him, and proclaimed it into this world of ours : This is God's beloved Son !

' Made perfect through suffering.' What ? Christ or His work ? Both. In Christ the subjective and the objective are united. Every step towards His perfecting as a Saviour was also a step towards the perfecting of salvation, and every progress towards the perfecting of His work was also one towards perfecting not His Person but His inner history as the Saviour. Some corresponding outward event in His personal life always accompanies every new stage towards the completion of His work of salvation.

I think I can obtain some glimpse of the reason of the remarkable reticence of Christ and of the Gospels about His Divinity. This reticence is the more striking that it stands in marked contrast to the utterances of the demoniacs on this subject, which were repressed, and the desire for its proclamation

by many whom the Saviour had healed, but whose
earnest wishes to announce His dignity are also
negatived. Why all this ? We are tempted like His
brethren to say, ' Show Thyself openly,' and to argue
that no man doeth these things and yet He Himself
remaineth hidden.

To say that premature announcements are un-
desirable is an answer without an explanation. So
far as the demoniacs were concerned, testimony from
such witnesses might indeed be unsuitable; but why
suppress it if it was, as it were, the almost involuntary
outcry of the demons, forced from them when brought
into contact with the Son of God ? More than that :
why were the demons so forward to make always such
confession ?

Whatever we may say by way of *ex post facto* argument, I am very sure we should in this respect have
expected and advised quite an opposite course had the
direction been left to us. What, then, is the explanation ?

Subjectively considered, or *quoad* the Person of
the Saviour, this reticence was part of His humiliation, His self-exinanition, His voluntary submission
to the ' no reputation.'

But objectively considered, or *quoad* His work,
this reticence was of the deepest importance. The

proclamation of His Divinity before the primary idea of His being the Saviour, the Healer, had taken deep root, would have been fatal. It would have overshadowed everything else, and engrossed the popular mind, dazzled it, so as to leave no room for the other. And yet, so far as we are concerned, the fact of His being the Saviour was primary, to which—with reverence be it said—that of His being the Son of God stands related only as the means to the end. It is not a selfish, only a true view, that with us the anthropological element dominates the theological. And so in the history of the Gospels it was those who had come to Him for mercy as the Son of David, for help and for healing, who, only *after* having experienced such, learned His power of forgiveness and His being the Son of God.

One evidence of the Divine origin of Biblical religion is, that it is not the religion of finality but of development. Every false religion is one of finality, it is from the first as at the end. The kingdom of God develops, as does humanity, as does life, from the smallest germ to final maturity—from the antediluvian stage of infant, or the Abrahamic stage of child-life, to the perfectness of Christ-likeness and reign with Him. It grows, and it grows *pari passu* with the life of humanity.

The real contest of Christianity is with the flesh, both experimentally and evidentially. So far as the latter is concerned, we have to encounter the materialism of nature and of history, the one represented by physicists, the other by 'higher criticism,' as it is called.

I have never read a book which so stirred my moral indignation as Renan's *Antichrist*. It is *Frenchism* in its truest and most odious manifestation. The sum-total of the book is that I am to despair not only of God but of humanity also. As there is no God in heaven, neither is there anything truly noble, real or genuine upon earth. There is delusion about heaven, and there is delusion upon earth. Our martyrs are miserable fools, and self-sacrifice of the noblest kind is prompted by the most egregious folly and deception. The profanity in reference to man is as great as that in reference to God. And the *residuum* left us is a Frenchman, a *boulevard*, a *café, eau sucrée, absinthe*—and *esprit*!

God help us, if this were the result of history !

If the Epistles of St. Paul were now to appear for the first time, I doubt whether a 'religious' publisher would be found to undertake them. Too lax, too doctrinal, too sectarian, too broad, not sensational enough—which shall we say? The 'Plyms' are at least sufficiently honest to tell us that they are 'beyond Paul's standpoint:' they need no confession of sin; use not the Lord's Prayer; would not have gone to the Temple; dared not appeal to Cæsar; approved not of centurions; would not ordain to the bishopric; appointed no elders in any place; would not allow each to be fully convinced in his own mind, far less observe or not observe fast and feast days; finally, strictly inquired of everyone, before admitting him to the 'love feast,' whether he had judged *Newtonism*, and was 'outside everything.'

There is unspeakable comfort in this Scriptural experience: 'Be not silent to me: lest, if Thou be silent to me, I become like them that go down into the pit' (Ps. xxviii. 1), with which also compare Ps. xxxv. 22 and cix. 1.

The two great difficulties in religion are: the mysteries of our faith and the inconsistencies of Christians.

The Gospel of St. Mark reads to me like the *primitive* record of the life of Christ, so simple, and as it were drawn from first sources. [It seems to me almost as if St. Mark i. 15 had been misplaced by a transcriber, and should stand after verse 4.] As you go on reading chap. i. the spiritual impression deepens, till you come to the story of the healed leper, when it is almost impossible not to make personal application both in regard to the sense of need and to the prayer for cleansing.

There is almost as great a difference between the Apostolic Epistles and the Synoptic Gospels as between the latter and the Old Testament. One instinctively feels that there must be a Book of Acts between them—that the outpouring of the Holy Ghost has intervened.

I cannot understand the history of Jesus Christ without that of St. Paul, nor yet that of St. Paul without that of Jesus Christ. It almost seems as if he at whose feet the witnesses who stoned the proto-martyr laid down their clothes, had caught the impress of the vision of St. Stephen, and reflected it into the world.

I dislike a book of ' extracts.' It is like giving a person a bottle of mixed pickles for dinner.

There are two kinds of immovableness—that of the rock, and that of the india-rubber ball, which takes every indenture, and goes back again to its old form.

A Christian is like a diamond, flashing many colours in the light of the Sun of Righteousness.

It is wonderful how many more people are bound to this earth by its cares than by its joys.

It seems to me that the true logical inference from ' prayers for the dead ' would be universal restoration or universalism. If the prayers of God's people— their mercy—can prevail for the mitigation, shortening, and removal of punishment in another world (if there be no moral barrier in the way), shall we believe that God's pity and mercy will not ultimately accomplish that which even His people's prayers can partially achieve ?

It is mostly with young Christians as with young

people. They are very intolerant of the blemishes, faults, annoyances and even wearisomeness of those whom they meet. As we get older and have wider knowledge of self and others, we come to put up with each other's failings and follies.

Upon the whole I have no hesitation in saying that the *Westminster Confession* is, in regard to the Sacraments, decidedly 'higher' that the XXXIX Articles. I do not mean to say that the Scotch Churches are so at this time—indeed, there are but a very few of their ministers who understand the theological import of that most carefully drawn document, their Confession. Most of the Scottish ministers —probably 99 out of 100—are downright Zwinglians, whose teaching is utterly repugnant to that of the Confession. In this, as in so many other fundamental Articles, they have so entirely departed from the ancient lines, that it is difficult to understand that it is still seriously expected of candidates to sign the old formularies.

I have passed from the Scotch to the English Church, and have not for one moment regretted the

change. The *changing* was, and is, most unpleasant,
but not the *change* ; that has placed me where all my
sympathies find most ample scope.

I am convinced of the historical Church ; I believe
in a national Church ; I prefer a liturgical Church—
and on these grounds I have joined the Church of
England.

To find the need of Reformation in the Church must
have been like discovering faults in your house that
require extensive alterations. A man pulls down his
house, and after that perhaps finds that he has neither
the brains nor the means to build another. A
second builds in its place a flaring modern villa, at
great cost and without any taste. I think I should
prefer to preserve the old castle or abbey (if I had
such) with all its valuable associations and historical
memories, and simply make what additions and im-
provements are necessary.

I can understand how people can object to this or
that *in* the Church of England, but scarcely how any
rational devout man can oppose the Church itself. If
your theological tendencies are conservative, here is a

Church that has been planted at the Christianisation of England, with all that is noble and grand in the old services, traditions and rites, and with all superstition and idolatry removed : the old historical Church reformed. If you are liberal, what Church allows such latitude, consistent with orthodoxy, as that of the XXXIX Articles ? If you are devout, what services and prayers are like those of the Holy Communion—or, in general, like those of the English Liturgy, which addresses itself so constantly to the Person of the Saviour, without, as too many others, ignoring the First Person of the Godhead ?

Revivalism is in danger of degenerating into a new heresy. The Father is spoken of as if He were merely an angry Deity who required to be propitiated by blood ; and as for the Holy Ghost, there seems no room for His agency, nor place for Him, except occasionally in the hymns and prayers. Then there is a—to me—terrible, wholly unscriptural familiarity with the God-Man about it all: a use of terms, comparisons and expressions which are not only wholly unscriptural, but antiscriptural, and even absurd and profane. I fear the reaction ; it will be to High-Churchism on the one side, and to levity

on the other. But God will keep His own remnant
true to the end.

Am I very uncharitable in supposing that a good
deal of Liberationism and democracy spring from a
principle kindred to that which led the woman who
had overlain her child to approve of cutting the living
one in halves ?

Shut the door of patience upon thy heart, lock it
with the key of hope, and in faith hand its keeping
over to Him Who is faithful.

Death, physically viewed, is the dissolution of the
union of vital forces.

A miracle implies one of two things : the non-
adequacy of an effect to its cause, or the incompatibility
of an effect with other known causations. Hence the
proportion (as Prof. Bain is reported) : the grey
matter in the brain thinks, would postulate a miracle,
seeing that the effect—thinking—is manifestly non-
adequate to its cause (grey matter). The effect
cannot contain more than the cause, since it is the

outcome of the cause; it is the minor of which the cause is the major—and the minor can never contain more than the major.

A distinguished Plymouthist lately described the Church in these words: 'Hitherto Christendom has been only busy first making Christians cripples, and then making crutches for them.' The alliteration is pretty, and I can imagine the smile of delight as busy pencils noted down the master-sentence. Yet in very truth a more blasphemous statement, or one more destructive of the bases of our faith, could scarcely be made. If that be Christendom, what is the Christ? If such be the Church these eighteen centuries, what comes of the promise: 'Lo, I am with you alway'? If that promise has so signally proved untrue, what comes of your historical basis of Christianity?

If the Church had to be invented in the nineteenth century, its invention seems to have no better ground than that of the miraculous coat, or of the very wood of the Cross.

We speak of 'joys departed, never to return.' And yet no real joy ever wholly departs, but leaves on the heart a sweet memory of peace. And is not the afterglow more beautiful even than the bright sunlight? Oh, to carry with us an afterglow of life into another world ! ~

Trials are God's veiled angels to us.

We ought to feel thankful quite as much on account of those prayers which God does not hear, as on account of those which He does hear. Both are answers to prayer, even if not to prayers.

What we call disappointments are only not God's appointments.

The question why the age of miracles is past—or, to put it in another form : why miracles recede before an advancing civilisation—seems to me capable not only of a theological and philosophical, but of an historical answer.

The theological reason would be that we are now in the dispensation of the Spirit.

The philosophical reason would be, that just as the highest manifestation of the Holy Spirit consists not

E

in inspiration—of which, indeed, mechanical inspiration marked the lowest stage—but in the indwelling
of the Holy Ghost with its spiritual influence, so the
highest motive power on our minds is not that produced by miraculous manifestations, but by the
personal determination and the willing subjection of
our spirits—the former being the result, as it were, of
force from without, the latter of grace within.

But the historical reason seems to me the most
evident. It is an entire mistake to suppose that in
olden times miracles were an extraordinary mode of
Divine teaching. It was one strictly adapted to the
times. For in those days the mind of Jew and heathen
alike was accustomed to the miraculous ; and, whether
in false or true miracles, really expected it. The
miraculous was not something strange or new, but
something looked for. The ancient world as much
expected an argument from the miraculous, as we
from the purely rational and logically evidential. But
advancing civilisation has changed all this, and
banished the miraculous from the sphere of ordinary
thinking. Accordingly, a miracle would now, logically
speaking, be a real interference, not only with the
course of nature, but with our laws and habits of
thinking. It can therefore no longer be God's mode
of teaching to us.

The Law and the Gospel have the same object: to produce in man conformity to the Will, and therefore the Image, of God. Their only difference lies in the mode by which this is to be compassed. In the Law it is by authority from without, which, considering our sinfulness, must fail, as it leaves our inner man unaffected; in the Gospel, by an inward influence upon our nature through forgiveness by Christ, and fellowship with God in Christ.

Asceticism is Stoicism with a moral purpose, only Stoicism; but happily not with a self-glorificatory, but a moral purpose.

True religion is objectivistic; sensational, subjectivistic.

We must coin new words if we have new thoughts, since words are the symbols of thoughts, the coin of intellectual commerce.

Many clever sayings are only logical catchpennies, logical alliterations, which have no more truth—that is, likeness to reality—about them than the alliteration ' bow-wow' has to the real bark of a dog.

E 2

For the German word *Haltpunkt*, the French
have *point d'appui*. Does not this mark the intellectual difference between the two nations? What to
the French is merely a *point d'appui* whence to
make a spring, is to the German a *Haltpunkt*, or
'Hold-fast-point.'

It seems to me unreasonable and inaccurate to
speak of a First Cause. Instead of that we should
rather speak of a First Causation. A First Cause is
in itself unthinkable. Behind the First Causation
the Christian sees a Person, which is not *causa* but
causans; the Materialist sees—I know not what. Any-
how, let us give up the expression: First Cause.

Some modern science has carried unbelief one step
nearer to the utterly irrational. What formerly was
Materialism, ought now to be called Accidentalism.

Are our modern thinkers really prepared to be
Accidentalists? Man, with what we call the physical,
mental, and moral phenomena of his being—a fortuitous concurrence of atoms; the Kosmos—a fortuitous concurrence of atoms; and, lastly, history—a
fortuitous concurrence of atoms! Can there be any-

thing more unthinkable than such an explanation of that which is seen ?

The moment you admit the sublime thought of an economy of Nature, Accidentalism becomes impossible. Even if you spoke (figuratively) of an unconscious cerebration of Nature, it would imply the existence of a brain as the central organ of such cerebration.

The ancient division into a Kingdom of Nature and Kingdom of Grace, or even into Nature, Providence and Grace, seems to me one-sided, and based on defective induction. I would rather speak of Nature and History—the latter including the domains of Providence and of Grace—if, indeed, these two may be separated, whereas they are really one, Providence including Grace. Nature is the manifestation of God ; History, the manifesting of God. Nature represents His Law; History, His Rule, which, however, is in accordance with His Law in its deepest sense.

And so Hebrew (which is the only theological language) has but two tenses: the past, which is still present, and the future, which is already present. The one corresponds to Nature, the other to History.

The Providence of God is a semi-heathen term ;
the Jews would rather speak of God's Providing than
of His Providence. There are no abstract terms
applicable to God, Who is the one great concrete
Reality. Abstractions are our poor human form of
conception.

Many of the fundamental principles of what is
called Darwinism must be true, and assuredly find
their counterpart in Holy Scripture. I name here
only : selection, the survival of the fittest, and
development. Only by development we understand
in history (viewed objectively) not the same as in
nature. In the latter it means addition unto, in the
former unfolding from.

If there is One God—may the hypothesation be
forgiven—there must be one plan for the All, and if
one plan for the All, then a grand unity : and this is
the deepest principle of any modern *Welt-Anschauung*
(world-aspection). [Or, you might reverse the reasoning, and so arrive at the conviction of the Being of a
God.]

The higher view of heaven is not reward, nor even

happiness, but fellowship with and conformity to God. And this higher view of heaven indicates the better fitness for it.

Nothing is so truly humbling as our over-estimate by others. It makes one feel as if a hypocrite.

Art, like Scripture, has this for its object: to make us see, through the actual and outward, the spiritual and therefore the truly real. It presents reality, but as that through which we look far away into the ideal, which underlies all, surrounds all, and gives meaning to all.

Cousin is very wrong in describing Pascal as a sceptic, because he passed through certain phases of deep and terrible questioning. A sceptic is not one who has had doubts and difficulties, but one who has them as his final state. Those twisted rocks and hills *are* not molten stuff, although they have passed through that stage, and so arrived at their present condition. A man who has never doubted or striven (which is moral doubt)—well, I do envy him in some respects, or at least his happy repose. But—Holland is, no

doubt, a very easy country for driving through : still,
I do not admire its scenery.

There must be an element of truth in Phrenology,
since, on the one hand, certain lesions of the brain
affect certain definite mental actions, and, on the
other, certain mental actions affect bodily organs.
Yet it does seem unreasonable to attach a mental
faculty to a certain small portion of the brain. May
it not be that the portions of the brain (phrenologically,
organs) are connected, not with the mental faculties,
but with the sensations, feelings and passions which
are reflectively but inseparably connected with the
exercise of these mental faculties? I can imagine
a portion of the brain connected with the feelings
excited by the imaginative faculty, or the memory, or
abstraction of thought, or with feelings of fear, or of
awe, and so on. In that case all brains would be
essentially or potentially the same, but differ in their
development according to the capability of the mind,
as exercising one or the other mental faculty it brings
into requisition, more or less, this or that part of the
brain which gives the correlative physical accompaniment of the moral act : just as everyone has the same
muscles, but one or other is developed according to

the use which a man makes of his arm. This would also account for these two things : the development of brain with the progress of civilisation, and what are called inherited faculties—or, more correctly, inherited development of the sensational accompaniment of mental faculties. But such sensational accompaniment is the necessary condition of our bodily existence, as without it the mind could not act upon the body, or action itself be impossible.

This might also help us to understand dreams—*quoad* their origin. For if there be such *nexus* between the mind and sensation, I can quite understand how a bodily state can excite certain thoughts.

What is wanting in dreams is spontaneity or progress—not progression—which are distinctive of pure mind ; as the touching of a key on the piano (by whatever means) brings out the musical note.

Let us not forget that, after all, to our present apprehension all highest truth must be cast in human forms, and that there is something higher and deeper beyond them. Our theology is but Divine truth, presented in human form. Even that primal truth of the Three Persons in the Godhead, or rather of their inter-relation, is presented to us in a form adapted

to the earthly and human.   There is higher truth
beyond it—only symbolised by the present mode of
our apprehending it.   ' Now we see in a glass darkly,
but then face to face.'

Is there not wide application of this—even to
such questions as that of Inspiration ?

Is all this heresy ?

We are almost as much indebted to the Providence
as to the Grace of God.   Nay, are the two not
essentially one ?

Two considerations give me infinite comfort : the
Incarnation of the Son of God, and the condescension
of God to every prayer.   When I feel troubled as to
whether that great God really attends to the small
concerns of such as we are, I think of the Incarnation
of the Son of God ; and when I feel troubled about
this great mystery, I fall back upon God's condescension to all men and all their concerns, however
infinitely small, as viewed in His light.   In both cases
the relief is absolute and unspeakable.

May we not suppose that the Incarnation of Christ
may have other bearings than upon our earth only ?

As regards miracles, our difficulties always lie in the details, not in the general itself. But is it not so in all other manifestations of the Divine, even in our daily lives ? [So in the history of the wilderness journeys.]

The Incarnation of Christ is the miracle of miracles. Given belief in that, and all seems easily intelligible. I can believe the most miraculous Introduction to such a drama.

Live slowly your life : its joys and its sorrows ; its toil and its rest. He must eat slowly that would digest well.

Whenever you come in books on sharply defined distinctions, arithmetically put, in which seemingly kindred subjects are distinguished by being contrasted, as if their differences were marked by almost crystal abruptness of outline (as by Renan in his *St. Paul,* or *Halachah and Haggadah*), you may rest assured there is a fallacy at the bottom, all the more dangerous that the form in which it is presented is so attractive —for, like children, we love the crystals. Intellectual differences run into each other, and there are no

abrupt chasms or crystalline outlines. It is with
them as with God's dealings in Providence, where the
Providentia specialissima runs by almost imperceptible
gradations into the *Providentia generalis.* And this is
the mystery of Providence, which can only be understood by faith.

The great difference between men and animals lies
in spontaneity, the power of personal origination.
This is what the Germans would call *Ichheit.* I
can originate a train of thinking or study ; the animal
must have the train of thinking suggested. On
this power of origination, spontaneity, *Ichheit,*
depends all intellectual and moral progress. On it
seems to depend even the origination and the very
faculty of language.

I do not believe in machine-made men, whose wills
are moulded by circumstances, because I am conscious
of mental and moral spontaneity — at least, the
power of it. This is 'the breath of life' which God
breathed into man, and the principle of his immortality.
This individualism constitutes him an individual—
indivisibles, if you like, as forming a totality of various
mental and moral elements, held together by that
band of *I.* Animals are not individualised, but living

branches on the stem of nature's life. Cut them off, and they are dead.

The moral wrong of lying consists in this : that it involves the loss of personal responsibility. A person who tells ' a story ' loses the sense of being personally responsible.

All our humanity centres in our individuality.
All virtue is the forthputting of individuality.
All sin is the surrender of individuality.

Christianity has two postulates (in which, perhaps, its difficulty lies). Faith in the fact that God is, which is the postulate for its dogmatic aspect ; and faith that He is the rewarder of them that diligently seek Him, which is the postulate of its practical aspect. Faith in the first will make miracles, prophecy, and the Incarnation rationally believable ; faith in the second will lead up to prayer and holiness.

The first of these is, however, rather of the intellect, the second of the heart, and in some respects the corollary of the first. Hence Apologetics should chiefly deal with the first proposition, and so with the most hostile force in Materialism.

Given belief in anything supersensuous—be it God or the soul—and we have Archimedes' *fulcrum* for proving Christianity.

Psalm xxviii. 1 is the Litany of faith.

We do not mark the real difference between development and unfolding. Man develops, God's purpose unfolds: it is all there from the first, and it only opens up to us in the course of our development.

Most of our sorrows are only such because of our partial knowledge of them.

There seems this essential difference between wit and pun, that the one regards the substance, the other the form of a saying. I would banish among puns not only all that depends on alliteration, but even a mere antithesis of expression.

In man's thinking, even that which springs from association may become spontaneous.

God mostly answers our prayers in the slow evolution of His grand Providence. Hence, answer to prayer may be immediate and yet long deferred. Thus prayer also implies the discipline of faith as its complementary element, and hence answers to prayer imply a moral and spiritual thing in us, so that it is not a mere act of power or favour on the part of God to which we appeal, but something which has faith not only for its spring, but also for its accompaniment.

One of the noblest spectacles is that of faith continuing unshaken in the midst of passionate prayers, seemingly wholly unanswered. Will anyone after that say either that there is not a moral element about prayer, or else that prayer unanswered may not be really prayer answered?

Sudden, what are called direct answers to prayer, belong rather to the sphere of the miraculous. The present dispensation is that of faith, not of miracles.

On trials being sent in the course of God's Laws : This brings us fatally near ultra-Calvinism; and yet there lies an essential difference here—that ultra-Calvinism points to it as an open door, and bids you go in and acknowledge, making it an article of creed, not a subject of belief—and there is a great difference between creed and belief, one being *objective*, the other *subjective*, one *credendum*, the other *creditum*. Ultra-Calvinism eventually resolves itself into a mechanical, though not quite stoical, yet unmoral impersonalism, which is an utterly impossible demand on the human heart. This other which I advocate is not an entering into the Temple, but a kneeling at its threshold with believing expectancy that somehow the great and the good resolve themselves into a higher harmony.

Mystery indicates the boundary-line on our horizon on which the mist rests—the haze within which something is. Hence the Sacraments are mysteries. That which is a mystery is that which is enwrapped in that haze, of which only the dim outlines, not the clear perception, come to our vision. So the 'mystery of piety' (Christ), and its opposite, 'the mystery of lawlessness' (Antichrist); so the 'mystery of our faith;' so the 'mystery of God's Revelation,' which from the beginning was hid (Eph. iii. 3–5; vi. 19); so 'the mystery of the Kingdom' (St. Matt. xiii. 11); so the mystery of God's counsel (Rom. xi. 25; 1 Cor. xv. 51); and so the mystery of the Sacraments. Strictly speaking, there is no Old Testament parallel to it, the nearest being in

the Apocrypha (Wisdom ii. 22). The רוא and the
סוד are rather the secret and enigmatic than the
mysterious.

The lawful affection which we entertain towards the
creature, cannot become sinful by increase of degree,
so that we must love less in order not to love wrongly.
Our love to God differs not in degree, but in kind, from
that which we might rightly entertain towards men.
The two occupy different provinces. Whenever and
wherever the two affections come into comparison, they
also come into collision.

Man may write God's facts in blood; he cannot
alter them nor wipe them out, not even with blood.
The Jews could not wipe out the fact of the Christ in
the Blood of Jesus, nor the heathen the fact of
Christianity in the blood of the Christians, nor yet
could the Christians wipe out the continuance of Israel
in the blood of the Jews. Let it be—Jehovah reigneth!

I know only of one thing that is really impossible:
' He *cannot* deny Himself' !
Does not even this prove that, of all realities, moral
realities are the most real?

F

As regards memory, it strikes me that its exercise depends mainly, if not entirely, on physical causes. Every fact of mental consciousness produces a corresponding sensation, and that sensation a brain-impression. In fact, I cannot conceive consciousness without sensation, and hence corresponding brain-impression. Consciousness marks the point where that which is without touches that which is within, and in turn that which is within affects (potentially, if not actually) that which is without: to use a somewhat different illustration, it is the spark when the steel strikes the flint—only the spark is never quite extinct.

But if the mental impression is always accompanied by a sensation, and brain (or physical) impression, I can understand some of the phenomena of ' memory.' I can understand why lesions of certain parts of the brain should lead to the forgetfulness of certain, or of all, facts of memory. For to remember, I must first reproduce the physical impression, then follows the mental sensation, and then the mental fact (the process is the reverse of the original mental impression), just as in the musical instrument I strike the note, then comes the sound, and then the mental impression.

I think I can thus also see my way how disease of

the brain is connected with suspended or disordered mental action. Also, how in proportion to health I may remember and think more clearly.

Also, it helps me in trying to understand the *rationale* of dreams. By some physical cause the corresponding brain-impression, then the mental sensation, to which it was, as it were, the mine (the powder-train, I mean) is roused, and so on.

But I am getting out of *Tohu-va-Vohu* either into clear light, or outer darkness!

A new motto for Commentaries:

    ' The deep saith, It is not in me.'

I am afraid if Belshazzar were to give his feast to-night, he would find a Bishop, a Dean, or at least an Honorary Canon, to ' say grace ' (what an expression!). And, no doubt, the reverend gentlemen would show excellent cause for what they were doing.

Hope consists of two elements—doubt and presumption: it is their combination and transformation.

St. Peter was the Apostle of hope—his whole life was a combination of the two elements of doubt and presumption ; his religious experience and preaching their reconciliation and transformation.

Faith occupies a lower standpoint, because it implies the standing afar off of not seeing.

Love is the highest of all, because it contains nothing of the negative—not the mental limitation of faith (not seeing), nor the moral limitation of hope (as implying an element of doubt), but is altogether positive and unlimited.

For myself, I cannot understand the rascaldom which underlies writings and lectures intended to make men atheists. If everything is only mud—including, of course, such writings and arguments—what can be the purpose of them ?   Only that of self-display, and, for myself, I do not admire even the largest accumulation of mud standing out from circumnatant mud.

But, viewing it otherwise : who would not feel inclined to kick out the man who came to convince you that your father had been a swindler, and your mother a dishonourable woman ?

Great God ! Are there men to whom it is matter

of sport and self-display to deprive others of all that
makes self and life not only bearable but noble ?

1 Cor. xv. 29.—This verse, which has received the
strangest (mis)interpretations, seems to me, as I read
it, plain and easy. The Apostle has been combating
the idea of *some Christians,* i.e. *baptized persons,* that
there is no resurrection ('How say some among *you,*'
v. 12). In answer to this he reasons as follows :

The resurrection of the dead is inseparably connected with the resurrection of Christ : if the former
is an unreality, so must the latter be ; if the latter is
an unreality, alike our preaching and your faith are
an unreality. But, first, your faith is *not* an unreality
(vv. 17–19) ; on the contrary, it is the most sure and
joyous reality (vv. 20·28). Secondly, those baptized
persons among you who deny the resurrection of the
dead, and by implication that of Christ, may be con-
victed out of their own mouths. Their conduct is in-
consistent with their reasoning ; it is meaningless,
even absurd. 'If the dead are not raised at all (and,
by implication, Christ is not raised), then what are they
doing that are being baptized ? It would be baptism
over a dead Christ. What is the meaning of being
baptized over the dead, if you are right in your idea

that the dead are not raised at all?   In this view the
verse should thus be rendered :

'Else [if otherwise than my above reasoning]
what shall they do [what are they doing] who are
being baptized over the dead [over dead persons ; what
an absurd ceremony, in such a case, baptism over a
dead Christ would be] if the dead are not raised at all?
For what, then, are they being baptized over ? '

Baptism *has* a meaning if the dead are raised, for
then Christ is risen.   But what is the use of your
being baptized if, as you argue, the dead are not
raised ?   Is there any sense in being baptized over
dead people ?

Mark in the interpretation of v. 29 these things :

1. The reasoning is general.   If dead people cannot
be raised, what is the good of baptism ?   Is there any
object in being baptized over dead people ?

If Christ is the risen and living Saviour, there is a
meaning in being baptized in relationship to Him ; but
then He is the firstfruit of all the dead, and your
theory is false.   On the other hand, if your theory
is correct, there can be no sense in being baptized
over dead people.

2. Mark the meaning of ὑπέρ (see Canon Evans,
in his notes on the passage in the 'Speaker's Commentary ').   It means ' over,' whether in a physical

or moral sense—'over the dead,' that is, in relationship to the dead, as it were over them.

In this view there is a peculiar light thrown upon baptism, and, indeed, on the Sacraments generally. Distinguish the subjective and the objective elements in the Sacraments. Subjectively, baptism is *over* Christ; objectively, *into* Christ. Subjectively, the Holy Supper is fellowship *with* Christ; objectively, the fellowship *of* Christ: the Eucharist looks primarily to . His death; Baptism to His resurrection—both are a remembrance, but only as the basis of that κοινωνία which is the common element of both Sacraments.

3. To return to 1 Cor. xv. There still remains a third ground of St. Paul's contention: If the dead are not raised and Christ is not raised, and our preaching is all an unreality, why do we thus expose ourselves to suffering, and why all our self-denial and labour (vv. 30–35)?—the whole winding up with an appeal of mingled moral indignation and earnest conviction.

As regards the eternal future, we see it mostly as through the driving rain of our dark winter's day, or through the blinding tears of our heart's agony.

Miracles are of chief value as the evidence of a communion between heaven and earth. This is the

principle underlying all revelation. All religions
proceed on some such idea. . . . A prophet as the
medium of Divine communion (Mahomet, &c.) . . .[1]
Evidence of this object of miracles in the story of the
paralytic (St. Matt. ix. 2, &c.).

What a false view is that mostly taken of prophecy and its fulfilment. The latter is looked upon
and judged as if it were a suit of clothes measured on
to fit exactly. This mechanical and totally unspiritual
view lies at the bottom of much disbelief and mis-
belief. I would consider the relation between prophecy and fulfilment as that between the ideal and
real. The form in which the prophecy is couched is
that of the prophet's present standpoint—the circumstances in which he, or the nation, or surrounding
empires are placed. He sees the eternal truth, the
ideal, introduced on the scene of the present. This
form is necessary if the contemporaries in whose
hearing the prophecy was uttered, were alike to understand it, or to derive from it lessons. It is also
necessary if the prophet is to be not a soothsayer,
nor a passive instrument (like Balaam) in prediction,
but to rise to the moral height of the prophet as the

---

[1] The notes here are partly illegible.

man of God. Thus prophecy is like type—a type in words—which ever rests on symbol.

If those Pharisees of critical truth had understood this, they would not have condemned the guiltless, nor, worse than the Jews, sought to pull down those sepulchres of the prophets which the Jews had built!

[1] So, our common parent, and that of the universe, our old friend Bathybius, is but Sulphate of Lime! Oh poor wretched humanity, springing from Sulphate of Lime! Oh great Kosmos, with all its intricate inter-arrangements and adaptations, but the outcome of Sulphate of Lime! Oh ye flowers, birds, animals, human beings, high thoughts, lofty moral aspirations, spiritual realities, all Sulphate of Lime! Oh grand evolution from primal Sulphate of Lime! Oh ye fools and slow of heart to believe, who worship a Bathybius, ideal Sulphate of Lime, and forget the Creator! God help us, with our pseudo-*e*volutions, and our slimy sin-and-unbelief *in*volutions!

And so it all comes back to this at last, which I

[1] The following remarks were elicited by the summary of a lecture of Dr. Jeffrey's sent him by a friend. Though probably dating about 1880, they are here introduced because their closing sentence fairly represents the position which the writer maintained, consistently with a deep and growing interest in the progress of science, up to the end.

have long believed to be the case, that our facts are as yet far too narrow—I shall not say for this or that conclusion, but for *any* definite system to rest upon.

What a terrible picture that of Judas! Once he lost his slender foothold—or rather, it slipped from under him—he fell down, down the eternal abyss. The only hold to which he clung in his fall was that one passion of his soul: covetousness. As he laid hold on it, it gave way with him, and fell with him into fathomless depths.

We, each of us, have a master passion. And if, which God forbid, we should lose our foothold, we should grasp this master passion, and it would give way, and we should carry it in our hand into the eternal dark and deep.

How utterly desolate must Judas have felt when the terrible storm of despair swept over his disenchanted soul! No one could have stood by him in that hour of utter despair. Not even the priests who had paid him the price of his treachery would have aught of him. And to this day not even the Synagogue would own or have him. I should like to ask the Synagogue whether they would own him: I am sure their answer would be: ' See thou to it ! '

Even if Judas had possessed that which on earth

cleaves closest to us—a woman's love—it could not have abode by him. It would have turned into madness and fled; or it would have withered, struck by the lightning-flash of that night of terrors.

Did Judas meet those searching, loving eyes of Jesus, Whose gaze he knew so well, when he came to answer for his deeds done in the flesh?

And—can there be a store in the Eternal Compassion for the betrayer of Christ?

The prophet sees the future in the light of the present, and the present in the light of the future: he wells forth of the waters of God, and he is the man of God. The one is prediction, the other prophetic preaching.

There are a number of people who advance—not by steps, but by *pirouettes*.

The Church is an ideal (yet very real) unity. It is the substantive of which believers are the adjectives.

I love the Church, but I detest your regular ecclesiastical personages.

The Gospels do not give us a ' Life of Christ,' but the ' History of the Christ '—that is, the presentation of Jesus as the Christ—each from its own peculiar standpoint.

It is wrong to say that prophecy or miracles—notably those of Christ—have a moral object or aim. Nothing of the kind. The Divine has no aim, or object, or ' scheme.' They have the *moral* as their characteristic element, not as their aim.

Our materialistic scientists are like children playing at the Kosmos, who would fain convert it into a gigantic mud-pie. *E pur si muove!*

No man is fit for greatness who has not got beyond vanity. May not this be the reason both of the failure of so many, and of the Divine discipline in regard to others ?

There are whose minds are like those walls in which you cannot fasten a nail. It seems difficult to know how the first principles of faith can be firmly fastened in them. I should say: In such cases make the moral element in Christianity the primary, and

the mental the secondary consideration. It was
thus that St. Peter—who seems to me rather to have
been of that disposition—conquered when the tremor
of universal doubt and mental difficulty had fatally
seized so many. St. John vi. 68, 69.

You must have felt in measure the agony of the
first, in order to understand the agony of the second
Garden.

Miracles would in our days be a moral anachronism
[morally an anachronism].

I greatly dislike certain theological commonplaces
which even good people use. One of these is 'the
scheme of salvation,' or 'the plan of salvation.' With
reverence be it said, God has neither scheme[1] nor plan
in salvation; it is the outgoing of Himself, Who is
Love.

It is a clever saying of the Rabbis (Pesikta R. 21)
that the commandments correspond to the ten creative

---

[1] [*Author's Note.*] I take the word *scheme* here in its ordinary
sense, not in that of σχῆμα, although even thus it would have no sense.

commands in Gen. i.   Thus the creative command of
the two great lights would correspond to the Fifth
Commandment, 'Honour thy father and thy mother.'

I like the Jewish combination and symbolico-
unification of the whole Old Testament—it is like a
codification of it.

I feel convinced that the real root of anti-Semitism
is depreciation of the Old Testament.   If we have low
opinions of the Old Testament we shall come to de-
spise and to hate the Jews, and perhaps not unreason-
ably so.   Love for the Old Testament leads to love for
Israel.

Whether or not men believe in Christianity, they
must admit that it has succeeded in surrounding with
brightness and glory that which under every other
form of thought or of religion has been most repulsive.
I am now specially thinking of the Resurrection.
Here the dead, putrefying body—the most abhorrent
of all things—becomes an object of interest, is sur-
rounded with the halo of glory.   The highest thought
of affection of which heathenism was capable consisted
in burning the putrefying body, that its pure ashes
might be with the survivors.   Christianity buries the

body, and teaches us that its putrefying death is the transition of the germ into the golden grain—that out of this putrefying body shall spring the Resurrection-body. This is the victory over the grave, and the very sublimeness of poetry as well as of religion. Mark also the sublimeness of the avowed contrast between the seen and the unseen in *burying* in the sure and certain hope of a blessed *Resurrection*.

With what body shall we rise ? Like or unlike the past ? Most like, yet unlike also. Our bodies will be *true*—for the soul will body itself forth according to its past history—impress itself not only (as now in the features), but express itself, so that a man may be known by what he is, and as what he is. Here it is, in one sense, the reverse process. All sensations, thoughts and actions leave, as it were, a permanent impression on the *sensorium*, or brain-matter. And these permanent impressions in part react on the mind, as we only too painfully know from the temptations of evil habits or imaginations. But there, the purified soul shall body itself forth—express itself, the same yet not the same : the same that it had been in this life, but purified, sanctified and perfected.

A speculation is the suggestion of a possibility.

And very useful may even a speculation be from the apologetic point of view. It suggests a possibility. Now an objection cannot be absolutely fatal if it can be met by a reasonable speculation. Even though it were not correct, it implies the *possibility* of an answer —hence the objection is not unanswerable, though it may be unanswered. That only is a fatal objection which involves the impossible.

The impossible—I mean mentally or morally. As regards the physical, we cannot say what is the impossible, partly from our partial knowledge of Nature, and partly because here there is another factor : God.

But the fact that as regards the mental and moral we can absolutely affirm that a thing is impossible, while we cannot do so as regards the physical, affords evidence that, as regards the mental and moral, man is God-born and God-kindred. It is the highest confirmation of the history of man's creation in Gen. i.

Providence is well put in the neuter gender, for when men and women will not help you they generally point you to *it*.

In the days of Christ men first believed in His

Person and then in His Message; in the dispensation of the Spirit we believe first in His Message and then in His Person.

'The miraculous' is only a relative and a subjective term. It is the to us unprecedented and uncognisable. In an absolute sense there is no miracle : something that has no preceding links in the chain of rational causation—an isolated phenomenon which has no *nexus* with anything around, before, or afterwards, but hangs alone and unsupported on the *fiat* of a Supreme Power. This is the common idea attaching to miracles. Against such coarse realism of the miraculous, philosophy is in many respects in the right—nay, the laws of our reason, which refuse to believe in an effect without an immediately preceding cause, and so on upwards to a final Cause, and even there (if we are Christians) places the moral purpose as the ground of the final ' I will.'

But I do not believe in this kind of supra-naturalism. It seems to me to destroy the moral order of things—the *Kosmos*—and to render any rational conception of the Divine government—nay, of the Divine itself—impossible.

I believe in the miraculous—i.e. in the directly

G

Divinely caused, not through a mere *fiat*, but through a series of natural causation. True—and this is characteristic of the miraculous—we are not able to trace, to perceive, and understand this series of natural causation. But none the less it is there. And here what are called miracles and what is called Providence—especially the *Providentia specialissima*—closely meet.

Quoad rem:—as God manifests Himself in creation and providence I would distinguish two kinds of miracles, according as they must be referred to either the one or the other. Thus I would consider the miracle of the manna one of creation; that, for example, of the quails one of providence.

By the side of these two I would place another kind of the miraculous (using the term again in its subjective and relative sense) : that of calling forth existing powers and forces and laws unknown to us, and which for certain reasons are not ordinarily exercised, or held bound. In this class I reckon Christ's walking on the sea, His command of nature, the flowing of Blood and Water from His Side, and even such miracles as the cleaving of the Red Sea or the arrestment of Jordan.

I repeat that it does not follow because I know not the natural *nexus* of these *phenomena*—their connection in the chain of natural causation—that such does not exist.

Why are preachers in the habit of asking a series of questions in the pulpit when they immediately add : These are questions which we cannot answer ? What can be the use of publicly asking a question which on your own showing you cannot answer ?

There is a subjective and an objective purport of prayer : subjective, to morally and spiritually influence us ; objective, with reverence be it said, to move the Hand that moves the universe.

There are two directions noticeable in the New Testament : that towards absolute freedom, and that towards asceticism. Though seemingly opposite, they run side by side ; and St. Paul tells us that one man may pursue the one, another the other (one man observes a day, &c.). What is it then ? Are they irreconcilable ? No ; but that the Gospel, being not a law from without, but a living principle—or rather a spring of life—within, assumes different directions according to the state and character of different men.

So that what asceticism is and effects in one man,
liberty does in another.

For, after all, the Law is not the final object, but
only means for attaining it (I mean, the Law in its
positive, not its negative aspect : the 'thou shalt,' not
the 'thou shalt not'). The final object is holiness
and growth unto God.

Most of our modern theology consists of casting
the grand old Jehovahism into Western mould—sub-
stituting logic for worshipful intuition and intuitive
worship. But, after all, those ideas belong to the
Isles of the West, where the sun goes down, not where
it rises.

We speak of God as the first great Cause—bah !
the Old Testament knows nothing of a 'first cause :'
it speaks of Jehovah, the Living God. We speak of
these three as the grand ideas of religion : devotion,
altruism, and enjoyment. The Old Testament sums
up theology in three words : *Leka Jehovah haarets
umeloak.* Here are the three grand ruling ideas of
the Old Testament : the Creatorship of God by His
Word simply—setting oneself above all mere second
causations, as scarce worth notice ; the proprietorship

of Jehovah, His immanence in and living *nexus* with earth and its fulness ; and the Reign of God.

All else flows from these three fundamental positions.

Hold fast by the unity of the Old Testament : not its connection, but its unity. You cannot perceive a mosaic by a little piece of stone.

I cannot understand the difficulty in recognising the Church as the unity of all the baptized. Surely its effect must be correlate (commensurate ?) to the cause, and the Church extend as far as the Redemption of Christ, which is for *all* men. The only thing required to be added is a profession of Christ.

I believe in a personal God ; I also believe in a personal Satan.

Agnosticism on the latter point seems to me to lay us open to the most serious practical dangers.

However we may speculate, we always come back on the great fundamental doctrines of ' the precious Blood of Christ ' and ' the forgiveness of sins ' in our hours of sorrow, distress, doubt and anxiety, and in death—not because they are the hours of our weakness, but those of our real need.

The difficulties in religion lie chiefly in matters of detail, not in fundamentals and principles. This alike as regards Apologetics and Dogmatics, and is very noteworthy.

I hate that kind of preaching which pretends to rearing mountains. In reality they are only children making 'mud-pies,' which they call 'mountains.'

Correct thinking is that which conforms itself to a certain standard : whether in the memory (of fact), in judgment (of reasoning), or in the moral faculty (of conscience). I do not think that animals have that power of bringing their thinking to such a standard : hence they are incapable of improvement or progress. Man, even the most sunken, has it—and with it the principle of improvability, which is the germ of immortality.

The more one studies ancient, especially Eastern,

history in its records, the more is one struck with
this as the result of Christianity: the deliverance of
the individual—the acknowledgment of individuality,
of individual dignity, of moral individuality and individual liberty.   Look at the Egyptian and Assyrian
monuments—think of Eastern notions even now, and
try to conceive the almost inconceivable change!
But it is on this basis of the moral *Gleichbürgerlichkeit*
of the individual as such—hence of equal rights [or
rights at all] and equal duties, that modern society is
based, and it is towards the full realisation of it that
civilisation, in its inward development and outward
progress, tends as its final goal.   Thus, Christianity
may well claim to be the founder of modern society
and civilisation in their ultimate basis and highest
aims.

But what of that which seems to contravene this
—in the persecutions which have followed, in the
religious wars which have been kindled, and even the
resistance which has occasionally been made to the
progress of science, and to liberty, in the name of
Christianity, and perhaps by those who loved it well?
I say, so far from disproving, they rather establish
the former position.   For they testify to the introduction of a new principle: new to men (from above),

and new to society ; and the presence of this twofold
principle must lead to a combat (in this respect
also : 'I came not to send peace, but a sword'), of
which these are the manifestations. Yet liberty and
civilisation must progress, because the new Divine
principle of individuality can make its appeal to, and
finds an echo in, man—whose moral nature is fallen
but not destroyed, and who therefore instinctively
responds (in his upward tending) to the Divine Voice
from without.

In the defence of the faith we have, indeed, one
great advantage over our opponents. Every Biblical
fact which we can prove serves *pro tanto* as presumptive confirmation (evidence?) of others ; while
every difficulty which they raise—unless indeed they
can prove it both fundamental and insurmountable
—to which no answer can be offered, only invalidates
pro tanto that one fact, but does not touch the rest.
And, even if it were insurmountable, i.e. if no
answer could be offered to it (and every attempt at
an answer indicates that a solution is not absolutely
impossible or unthinkable), unless you were to show
me that the difficulty was so fundamental as to
involve the whole argument, you would only force me
to modify my view of inspiration—i.e. not me, for I

do not hold the mechanical theory of it, but those who believe in a verbal inspiration.

On this argument it almost seems to me as if a new 'Butler's Analogy' could be constructed.

Let me give an example. Supposing you proved that Samson's history were not real, or any other recorded narrative, it would not invalidate my faith in the Bible itself. But supposing I proved to you any fact, say (as Dr. Kinns proposes) that the fifteen creative steps recorded in Genesis are in exact accordance with geology, I should have a *fulcrum* by which to prove the whole Bible to be the Revelation of God. So, if I proved the Resurrection, I should have also proved the miraculous Birth; or, if one miracle [though in the nature of things *proof* of a *miracle* seems a contradiction in terms], I should have presumptively proved all. And in some minor degree this applies even to smaller facts. Every Biblical fact corroborated, for example by the Monuments, carries support to the others.

One step more. It seems that every fact of Negativism disproved causes a fatal breach in its walls which cannot be repaired.

It may be—and this continues the argument of the new 'Analogy'—that there are many unresolved

questions about Revelation.   But then it is a question
of probabilities : where the greater balance lies.   And
I think there can at least be no doubt that the greater
probability rests on the positive than on the negative
side, and that the latter involves far more difficulties
than the former.

And here it must again be recalled that every
Gospel-fact established, every miraculous event confirmed, affords presumptive evidence—and that of the
strongest kind—of the others.

In fact, *one* miraculous event established, or, re-
membering that miracles are part of the humiliation of Christ, one supra-naturalistic (not necessarily
supernatural) fact established, and by proving mira-
culousness you have proved your whole case.   If *one*
miracle, if *one* supra-naturalistic fact in the Bible is
true, the Bible is true.   It may be that some of the
accounts are not exact, even mistaken ; it may be that
criticism will take from us much ; but the *general drift*
of the Bible, its direction for us and to us, must be
true and reliable, and it must be a real and direct
Divine Revelation, if *any* part of it is directly from God.

You must therefore prove *the whole* to be false
before you make out your case.   And if the case is
thus put, in which direction does the balance of probability lie ?

It is quite true, as some of my critics have said, that there is a difference between not being able to account for the origin of a narrative and believing in it. I may not be able to account for one of the Gospel accounts of miracles &c., and yet it may seem and be incredible. But our opponents are not stating the case fairly. These are not like ordinary legends, such as of Romish saints. You have here: first, the previous existence of an opposite opinion in Jewish (contemporary) expectancy. Secondly, you have—and I here confine myself to such narratives—the *consensus* of three or four Evangelists : separate, independent witnesses, and, on the theory of negative criticism, of different and even opposing fundamental tendencies, where divergence, not *consensus*, would be expected. Thirdly, you have here not details, which would be regarded as embellishments, but fundamental principles, on which the belief, nay, the existence, of the Church was historically grounded. Take here, for example, the Resurrection (the argument in its favour from Pliny's account is very striking).

Now I maintain that in view of these three facts, negative criticism is bound to offer us some reasonable explanation of the origin of this *consensus* in regard to the miraculous events in the life of Christ.

People argue very strangely in regard to the fulfilment of prophecies—or rather, to their application
to Christ. It is supposed that the person who spoke
the prediction—often even that those who first heard
it—must have understood its full meaning; or at
any rate its Messianic bearing, or at least have had
the full conception of a personal Messiah as we
Westerns now have it. So, for example, Gustav Baur,
in his very thoughtful and learned *Gesch. d. Alttestam.
Weissag.* generally, and specifically in regard to ' the
last words of David' in 2 Sam. xxiii. But the premisses
are by no means true. It does not follow that the
prophet—still less his hearers—had a clear or a full,
in some sense perhaps even a partial, knowledge of
the Messiah and Messianism as in the light of
completion we now perceive it. In fact, such would
be simply impossible. For (1) It would set aside the
historical development, which is both the rational
order and God's order. (2) In its stead it would
introduce a mechanical and externalistic view of God's
revelation, similar to that which in Theology introduced the fatal notion of a mechanical mode of
inspiration, and the literal and verbal inspiration,
and in natural science (viewed from the theological
standpoint) scouts the idea of development, and views
all as finished and ended from the beginning—a view

which has been the bane of much that might otherwise have been saved in Natural Theology and in
Apologetics, and on which the old—I would say coarsely
realistic-supranaturalistic has been wrecked, involv-
ing in its fall, alas! much that is true, and must
now be dug out of its ruins and built up again—the
builders having now, like the men of Nehemiah, to work
with the sword in the one hand and the trowel in the
other. (3) It would eliminate the moral and spiritual,
the teaching and advancement, from God's Revelation.
(4) It would render all future prophecy needless,
since everything is already clearly and fully there, and
understood by all. (5) Lastly, it is in direct contrariety
to the principle underlying 1 St. Peter i. 10, 11.

On the other hand, I would maintain that in
truth *prophecy can only be fully understood from the
standpoint of fulfilment.* The principle seems, indeed,
one of common sense, since otherwise prophecy would
cease to be prophecy, and become simply foretold
historical narrative. But if this were the object, it
would obviously have been far better, it would be
more rational (*sit venia verbis*), since it would have
served the purpose better, to have said it out plainly,
without figure or metaphor—in language that could
not have been either mistaken or misinterpreted.

And so certain dull persons in our time would have

it not only in regard to prophecy of old, but they also bitterly or else querulously complain that the New Testament should have told us everything plainly, giving us every clause and particular, down to the minutest direction as to the modes of our organisation, the direction of our bodies, and the very angle of our genuflexions. But it is not so, it never can be so, if, as we believe and know, our religion is of God.

There are, indeed, some excellent people who will take the exactly opposite standpoint, and will give us, once for all, a precise and authoritative answer to every possible and impossible question— and their doxy is orthodoxy : all else, all reference to the *Zeitgeist* and its promptings, is unfaithfulness to the truth and rationalising. Now you may direct the *Zeitgeist* and its tendency, but you cannot bind it, nor cast it out, least of all with your formulas. It is a foolish and ignorant Delilah who would bind Samson with withes, new or old. You only do harm to your cause. For Samson will shake himself, and not only burst your bonds, but carry away with him the gates of your Gaza. It is not from impiety or rationalising that we insist on the new application of the old truth, on the new wine being put into new bottles. Christianity is always new : it has something

new to say to every new generation, though the new
be always the old truth. And therein lies its appeal
to our times.

What in their demands is true and reasonable
has been granted, though not in their foolish way.
History has taught us what the New Testament
contains; and the enlightened Christian consciousness
has learned to read—has, as in bilingual inscriptions,
learned the characters and the language in which
much of the past is written. History has unfolded
much that the New Testament had infolded, and the
enlightened, observant, Spirit-taught Christian consciousness has learned to perceive and understand it.
Let it not be said : Then were they of old ignorant
in measure of the truth. It is not so ! In measure—i.e.
in their measure—they were *not* ignorant of it, but
knew it. But then their measure is not our measure.
I believe in this sense in advancement and in progress.
Divine truth and revelation is indeed one, full and
final, and nothing can be added to it. But with the
development of our wants, with the progress of our
progress, its meaning unfolds, and it receives constantly new applications. We understand things
more fully—if you like, differently from our fathers—
not because these things are different from what they

had been, but because we are different from our
fathers; because questions have arisen for us which
had not come to them; because events, mental and
moral, press upon us which had never presented
themselves to them. *It is not the old truth which is
different: it is its application,* as we witness the
unfolding of the old truth; and from its adaptation,
ever fresh, ever new and ever true, to all times, to all
men, to all events, we gather fresh and living evidence
of its Divine origin.

[Confirmation from the inapplicableness of old
sermons—I have read most of the Puritan divines and
Jonathan Edwards. In morals — see the slave question.]

Long as this digression is, you will perceive its
application to the study of prophecy and of its interpretation. I repeat, that prophecy can only be fully
viewed from the standpoint of its fulfilment. Prophecy
is a life-germ: it contains all that the full truth has, and
yet it contains nothing of it. What prophecy infolds,
history unfolds. And so we find that, with the ex-
ception of the prophecy of Christ's Birth at Bethlehem,
prophecy is never pointed to in the New Testament,
except in regard to its actual fulfilment. Accordingly,
it was only *after* His Resurrection that Christ on the
way to Emmaus opened up the Scriptures of the Old

Testament to His disciples, and showed them the application to Himself of what Moses and all the prophets had written—although He had previously indicated this when (in St. John) He pointed to Moses as testifying of Him, and when He silenced His cavilling adversaries by asking them to solve the riddle of Ps. cx. which could only be read in the light of its actual fulfilment.

The religion of Revivalism is too often like an apple roasted at a quick fire : soft and pulpy outside, hard and sour inside.

Most people's minds are so coarsely constituted that they dwell exclusively upon miracles : they are either their great evidence for Christianity, or else their great objection to it. Now, as regards Christ Himself, apart from this, that they were a necessary outcome—and hence a necessary condition—of His Theanthropism (out of His fulness He must pour forth, and He could not be brought in contact with disease, death, sin, without banishing it), I feel convinced that as condescension to the standpoint of His contemporaries they formed part of His humiliation.[1] Even as the means of legitimatising

[1] (*Author's note.*) ' How long shall I be with you—how long shall I bear you ? '

H

His claims [and this is the coarsely supra-naturalistic view of miracles] they were part of His humiliation. Even we—that is, every noble-minded man—feel it a deep humiliation, something that makes us feel poorer (a self-exinanition : and is not humiliation always exinanition ?) to have to prove by outward deeds what we inwardly and really are.

But that which is of chief value in miracles is the miraculous considered as evidence of a communication between heaven and earth. Such a communication is the postulate of all religions—hence perhaps the miraculous in all religions : in some coarsely, in others refinedly; in some congruously, in others incongruously, to the thing—according to the intellectual standpoint in each.

But such communication between heaven and earth is not only the postulate in all religions—it is also the postulate of Theism. If there be a God, and we His creatures, it follows that there must be such communication : because He is what He is (not a *Roi fainéant*), and because we are what we are (moral beings, in His image, and with natural and necessary aspirations after Him).

But this communication is of twofold kind : Revelation and miracle—communication by word or by deed : revelation is a miracle by word ; miracle is a

revelation by deed. And to each there is an analogue
in another and lower sphere (as sleep is of death).
The analogue to the miracle is Providence (hence
miracles are only *Providentia specialissima,* and
between the two it is not easy practically to ride the
marches); the analogue to revelation, the conceptions
of genius.

It is a fallacy to suppose that age brings wisdom
or knowledge. The lapse of time adds nothing to our
potentiality, it only develops what is in us. At the
age of sixty a man is either a perfect fool, or he ought
to have a good deal of sense.

It is with the mind as with the body. If a man
has much physical life in him, it exuberates and flows
over, often in naughtiness [in the shape of false con-
clusions, rash inferences, &c.].

I do not blame our philosophers for accentuating
so much the physical side of man and of the Kosmos.
It is there, and they see it. But I do blame them for
overlooking the other series of facts, the moral facts.
You say, the two seem contradictory, and you cannot
combine them! Be it so; but then, pray, why seek

to combine them ?   Let it alone, and learn that there
is body and spirit, and that the earthly is the Divine
combination of the two contradictions, till death them
do part.

I glory in it, that there are questions to which
no answer can be returned.   It shows that there is
something above earth and man.

I was yesterday at a *Scientific Conversazione,* which
much pleased and still more interested me.   Yet I could
not help feeling that these men were as children playing
at the shore of the eternal sea, where there are many
things beautiful and wonderful exceedingly.   But the
while they are so engaged with it all as not to
remember, if indeed they have the capacity for thinking of, the higher business of life.

And it does appear most instructive to me, how
these people try to *ablauschen* to Nature her secrets,
and by what flatteries and dodging they seek to coax
or to win them out of her.   But Nature is absolutely
silent.   For she has only one word to say to them :
God—and to that word they will not listen.

But quite as painfully grotesque are many of our
theologians.   When they get hold of a scientist—

mostly of the ill-baked kind—they parade him on all
their platforms and pulpits, as if he were a flat-nosed
Mongol, or a slit-mouthed savage. *Non talibus armis,
nec tali auxilio* did the Gospel of the Christ, when borne
by the living faith of the early Church, make its way
to the throne of the world.

Two things would I seek, and towards them does
His teaching in sanctification lead : *here*—faith ; *there*
—sight.

To the interested observer the question—not without great difficulties besetting it—frequently presents
itself : whether the exegete is only a scientific student
or also a theologian. In one aspect of it, it may
resolve itself into this—whether the man of science
can divorce himself from the personal element of
humanity, from share in it and sympathy with it ; in
short, can or should seek to become impersonal.
Whatever answer may be given to it in consonance
with the instincts of our human nature, which after
all cannot be wholly suppressed, the question wears a
somewhat different aspect as regards theology and
theological science. Theology and the theological
interest cannot be divorced from exegetical science.

Exegetical science exists for the sake of theology, not
theology for the sake of science. *That* is the end;
this only the means to it. Take away the real interest of theology, and exegetical science is no longer
worth cultivating except for the sake of its historical and antiquarian interest, and as a collateral and
subsidiary branch of comparative mythology. But
Kronos must not eat up his children. To us who
believe in the reality of religion—to whom it is matter
of the heart and of conviction : a question of life or
death ; to us whose heart-pulses beat in accord with
the great heart of humanity in longing for assured
fellowship with the Father; to us to whom Christ is
the great Reality, the Truth, the Way, the Life—
these are not matters of mere scientific curiosity : they
touch the question of life. We cannot separate
scientific inquiry in theology from theology as the
presentation of truth and of life. . . .

It is quite true that when advanced science has
reached its goal it commits suicide; when it has
proved that there is nothing in Christianity, it has
also proved that there is no need for theological
science. But the heart of humanity forbids this: it
rises in rebellion. If you take away Christianity, you
take away that which is most holy and most gracious ;
you extinguish the light that lighteth every man ;

you quench the one hope of humanity; you remove
the one great Ideal; you leave this world empty of
God—the play of accident or the prey of cunning
and brute-strength; you leave it, except for a short
time and for a few lucky ones, the most miserable,
dreary place.

On the other hand, science has its paramount
claims [so long as you do not forget that in one
aspect it is a means to an end]: they are the claims
of truth and the fascinations of knowledge.

To combine the two—never to lose sight of the one
or the other, yet to hold them in due proportion, such is
the rule of the serious inquirer, who on the one hand
recognises the Divine reality of religion, and on the
other the sacred claims of truth.

La-ti-tud-in-ar-ian-ism is a beautiful solid word of
many syllables, whereby many adversaries have been
chased, and some even slain. But I do not apprehend
the one, and I fear not the other. Yet I fear lest in
any way I should hurt the weak, whom I would rather
comfort—and so offend against what is the primary
law of Christ: Love.

Oh, that self should ever cast its shadow across

the path ! How *can* ye believe who seek honour one
of another ?

In all work for Christ—but especially in Jewish
work—what we need most is pity from love, not love
from pity.

What are called strong natures are mostly only
strongly self-conscious natures.

He is great who is great in small things and on
small occasions.

Our religious differences mostly spring from what
all of us do not know, but pretend to know.

Our friend —— is the Whiteley of Theology, the
' universal provider ' of astonishingly cheap wares.
And yet there is large profit from the goods, so that
they must have cost very little originally.

If you whittle away the distinctive doctrines of
Christianity, I do not know that Christianity is worth
defending. For, in that case, it would be at most
an historical interest that we attach to it, and not a

present one : what Christ *was*, not what He *is*, since
in any true sense He is not any more.

If you whittle away the distinctiveness of the
Christian life, I do not know that the Christian
religion is worth adopting. At most it were a
series of dogmatic statements, which have interest
for schoolmen, not for souls that long for God. No
one will get holy over the Athanasian Creed—fully
as I believe it : that is, so far as I understand it.

The modern Synagogue hates St. Paul as much
as the ancient Synagogue hated Jesus Christ. This
affords, I think, proof that he was a true Apostle.

What think ye of Christ ? Even if we were to
concede to Jewish controversialists that parallels for
all Christ's teaching are to be found in one or other
remote corner of a Rabbinic saying, in the course of
the centuries that preceded and followed the time of
Christ (as we find them collected in the Talmud), it
would not prove that Christ had derived them from
the Rabbis. For, surely, it could not be argued that
the Son of the carpenter-home in obscure Galilean
Nazareth had known and made the very substance of

His teaching what it requires the utmost ingenuity of special pleading to find *alluded to*, not spoken, in some isolated Rabbinic utterance.

In truth, the historical Christ is the best evidence of the truth of what Christianity teaches about His direct God-mission: that alone solves the historical difficulty of His history, as well as the historical problem of the new birth in the individual and in the Church.   In that new creation Christ was the first-born of many brethren: in this also He was the Virgin's Son.

Delitzsch beautifully says: the types are outlined sketches of the Christ—copies of which He is the original.

Israel is a suffering people, and even in its suffering essentially embodies the idea of the Christ as the Sufferer—the Sufferer for others.   If Christ had been no more than the Sufferer, He would have truly summed up in Himself Israel His people, and thus been their Messiah.

Modern Israel is fast losing all its poetry by losing its meaning.   The coarse plutocracy of the one set,

and the self-asserting conceit of the other, are cari-
catures most sad to behold.   There is utter loss of
pathos, utter loss of dignity, in all this tinsel-dress ;
horrible screeching in all this crowing with outstretched
neck.   There is Divine dignity in suffering ; only
ludicrous posing, to the exposing of all weakness, in this
maniacal shout of them of 'the Jewish persuasion.'
To me the sublimeness of Judaism is far better represented by the ' old clo's-man ' than by the West-end
' gentleman ' or the *naseweise* German Rabbi.

How can you forget the charter of your nobility by
forgetting Jerusalem, and singing to bad Gentile tunes
the songs of Zion by strange waters ?

Jew and Christian as I am, ' Missionary Meetings '
are becoming odious to me.   The benevolent pity over
the poor Jew, by those who neither know nor can
sympathise with him, my soul abhorreth.

The whole history of Israel before the Incarnation
of Christ may be divided into four periods :

1. Unconscious prophecy in Law and History [The Torah].
2. Unconscious life in the Church [The Kethubhim].
3. Unconscious predictions of the unrealised Ideal [Ne-
    bhiim].
4. The period of silence and the sorrows of birth.

Natural science speaks of development and evolution up to *man*; revealed *scientia* of development and evolution up to *God*.

It seems to me that Ecclesiastes may be a discussion or an essay, in later style and mode of conception, upon what really was, or else was considered, a Solomonic text (or it might be a summary) : 'Vanity of vanities, all is vanity.' And for this view there is also philological confirmation in the wording of that text.

The moral of the Book of Ecclesiastes is : *personal responsibility.* This as opposed to seeming (empiric) accidentalism and theoretic fatalism.

The account of creation in the Book of Genesis is neither a scientific essay, nor even a cosmogony, nor yet a moral presentation of it. It is simply a Divinely presented panorama, which successively passed before the view of the inspired historian. This does not exclude that he had in his mind those general cosmogonic conceptions—or, more accurately, facts (however first received)—which are common to all nations. Only the one great Factor in this cosmogonic panorama was *God*—and its *theologumena* are : the *fiat* of

God, and the living connection resultant from it between God and the *Kosmos*, with man as its climax.

The more we recognise the element of contemporary reference in Isaiah (as to Cyrus &c.) the more marvellous appears the Divine transformation of these elements in their generalisation and spiritual application in the picture of the Messiah and the Messianic Kingdom.

The chief interest in the Book of Sirach lies in this: that it marks a period, alike in an historical, literary and theological sense. It forms a middle and connecting link between the *Chochmah* books of later Hebrew canonical literature and Alexandrianism. It is the outcome of Grecianism in its gradual and yet unopposed influence upon Palestinianism. It precedes the period of antagonism, and may be regarded as one of those utterances which, as indications of the threatening *Zeitgeist*, provoked that reaction which evoked what afterwards developed into Pharisaism, and in turn evoked Sadduceeism. But it is pre-Sadduceeism. It existed before there were Sadducees, nay before there were Pharisees, even before there

were *Chasidim.* The latter as a party afterwards
merging into, or giving place to, the Pharisees, date
from before the Maccabean rising. The composition
of the Book of Sirach must therefore date before that
period—probably more than half a century—at any
rate before the year 200 B.C.

The party to which reference has been made must
have arisen in peaceful times, when the influence of
Grecianism, introduced through the world-reign of
Alexander the Great, was still unopposed, perhaps
even unsuspected. They professed to appeal to
Solomon, and the 'Wisdom' teaching of Hebrew
canonical literature which passed under his name.
When the opposite party arose they appealed from
Solomon to David, and took from the Psalms the
title *Chasidim* (Ps. xxx. 5; xxxi. 24; xxxvii. 28).
It may have been that while the party-name
Zaddaqim, afterwards taken in opposition to the
Pharisees, arose from the distinction between 'the
righteous' and 'the separatists' (*Perushim*), it also
applied to Simon I., the *Zaddiq*, the mild and pious
priest, who conciliated Alexander the Great, and might
be regarded as the representation of the *via media.*
If these views are correct, they would seem to confirm
the idea that the Simon of Ecclus. was Simon I., and
not Simon II., under whose pontificate a *via media* no

longer existed—indeed, would have been impossible. And further, if the Book of Sirach represents the yet unopposed admixture of Greek elements with Palestinianism, before such questions became party cries, and if in the Book of Sirach we have the Palestinian roots of Alexandrianism and Hellenism, it seems impossible to ascribe the date of its composition to the time of Simon II.

There is yet another point very noteworthy. From the older Sirach to the Epistle of St. James there seems a very long step. Yet we mark two things : 1. The constant correspondence between that epistle and the Book of Sirach. 2. That epistle itself seems to occupy a position analogous to that of Ecclesiasticus. Thoroughly Palestinian, it has many elements of Hellenism—is, indeed, a *via media* ; marks the stage when Judaic and Hellenic Christianity were still combined, undivided, non-antagonistic.

The chief use of books—excepting such as communicate simple facts, and may therefore be styled the Grammars of Science—is to lead us to think for ourselves on the subjects of which they treat. More than this few books yield—less than this scarcely any.

So then in a sense all books are useful or useless. That, after all, depends on the reader. There are many who 'cram,' few who read.

In Christ miracle has become permanent; in Christianity miracle (has become) has passed into history.

We fail to grasp the sublime thought of the Old Testament. It is: Prophecy fulfilled in Christ, because the Kingdom of God has become reality in the Church Catholic.

Christianity needs not any apology. Apologetics are one of our human impertinences. Christianity only needs a wider conception of the character and ways of God—and an open heart to receive it.

In truth, all our *knowledge*, in the strict sense, is *historical*: except such knowledge as is either based on axioms or on our laws of thinking.

When Professor Harnack (*Dogmengesch.* p. 50, note 4) writes: 'The historian is not able to *count* with a miracle as a certainly given historical fact,' he utters a truism, which might indeed be applied to any other fact recorded in history. When he adds: 'For thereby he [the historian] renounces [*aufhebt*] the mode of consideration [*Betrachtungsweise*] on which all historical inquiry rests,' he speaks words high-sounding but superficial.

History has to do with the *verum*—with fact: the *a priori* considerations which we bring to bear on the inquiry whether what is reported be fact or legend belong to the domain of the *verisimile*. When the spiritualist reports transmundane apparitions and communications, the historian rejoins by objections derived from the *verisimile*. And yet if the *verum* in these matters were established, the *verisimile* would have to yield. In point of fact, all preliminary presumptions, being originally derived from, and generalisations within, the domain of the empirical, must in turn yield to that experience of which themselves were the outcome.

Truth to say, history has no prepossessions, no antecedently binding law of negation: only cautions, queries. Its laws of evidence are internal, not external: its reasoning is *a posteriori* rather than *a priori*. To say that a thing is antecedently impossible, is to reason in a vicious circle. That only is impossible which is unthinkable. Historical inquiry

I

is inquiry into what is history—not an *a priori*
assumption that it cannot be history.

The miraculous in the Bible must be studied from
the standpoint of the historical Christ—just as prophecy must be studied from the standpoint of fulfilment, not of utterance. If the Christ can be proved
to be the God-sent, then the miraculous has become
history.

Perhaps the following may be canons for dis-
tinguishing legend from history :

1. Sufficiency [adequacy] of historical testimony.

2. An internal historical *nexus*.   The event recorded is not merely sporadic, phenomenal, but
stands in internal connection with the past, forms an
integral member in the organism of the present, is a
living element in the formation of the future. All
these are the necessary conditions of history. The
Resurrection of the Christ answers not only to the
first, but also to all the three requirements of the
second canon. A dead Christ could not have been
such as He historically lived ; nor could He have been
the foundation of the Church. A dead Christ could
not have become the life of a dead world : the water
cannot rise above its source. Besides, as regards the
Resurrection of Christ, we have also to reckon not
only with the utter absence of expectation, but with

the positive disbelief of all the disciples. And the presence of *a priori* objections in the minds of believers appears even from the reasoning of St. Paul in 1 Cor. xv.

The Resurrection of the Christ rules all the other miracles. When Harnack says: 'Every individual miracle remains historically quite doubtful,' he forgets that miracles are not each of them individual and isolated, but are all historically connected and a unity.

3. As a third canon I would state : Harmony with otherwise established historical facts and elements [i.e. facts which have passed beyond the sphere of the merely phenomenal—mere fact—into the permanently active—into lasting powers (*Triebfedern*)].   Or, to put it negatively, there cannot be essential contrariety between a reported fact and an historically established fact; or else, with one of the established active elements, which go to the formation of future history.

People speak of consistency in an exceedingly strange manner. They extol and worship it as another god [being a kind of self-adoration], while in truth it is the worship of the god stupidity.

There is a threefold consistency which is worthy of praise: (1) that inward consistency which is the

harmonious accord—the symphonium of a morally
concordant nature; (2) that outward consistency
which is the accord of action with the inner condition; (3) there is that historical consistency of harmonious development, which marks a deepening,
widening process in the progress of the inner and
outer life—true to its inner spring and true to its
outer manifestation. Yet on this point I have some
doubts, at least as regards uniformity of progress.
Life—if real, even if beautiful—is not the straight
course of a canal through an interminably flat country;
but rather like the Jordan, fast-flowing in its descent
and with many windings. I do not much admire
your pretty faces with perfectly straight hair. He that
has capacity for much rising has also the possibility
of much falling near him. He that cannot laugh
will not weep.

But, apart from this, what people generally call
consistency—the continuance in a course of action,
thinking or believing, whether because we have been
born to it or because we are placed in it through outward circumstances—is an exceedingly low thing. It
is persistency rather than consistency, it is mechanical
rather than moral. Such consistency is the outcome
of either stupidity or ignorance. It is the philosophy
of a vegetable: I am because I have been; I grow

what I have been planted. Yes, if you are vegetable. Such consistency excludes either all learning, or all capacity for it.

Strangest of all objections to Christianity seem to me those founded on morality. A religion that at its birth has been attended by the angelico-human choir of martyrs chanting their trishagion Christmas hymn of a new day on a world of heathen night ; a religion that has produced that moral miracle, a Christian slave ; a religion ushered in by the hymn of Bethlehem's plains ; a religion of which the first utterance is, ' This is the will of God, even your sanctification '— this religion is attacked on the ground of morality !

And by whom ? By those whose principles make the very idea of morality impossible. For their fundamental principle is the denial of free-will, that we are what heredity and circumstances make us. But then morality is impossible ; progress is impossible ; and inasmuch as the heredity of evil and the evil circumstances must naturally tend to spread and finally to be absolutely coextensive with humanity, since there is no possibility of a moral uprising, the outlook is into pessimism. Thus this school points to despair ; while Christianity, with its constantly upraising force, points to regeneration and moral victory.

The outlook of Positivism is into an earthly Pande-
monium ; that of Christianity into a Kingdom of God.

But it is said that such admittedly great person-
alities as, for example, Sister Dora, would have been
great even if they had not been Christians. This
ignoration of facts which are admittedly empirically
connected, is another instance of their *laches* óf
reasoning. What is meant is not that their lives
have another explanation, but that they may have
another explanation. This supposed possibility is
straightway converted into an actuality, with no better
support than that it has occurred as a possibility to
the brain of a speculant. And you call this reasoning! What in my opinion *may be*, that in point of
fact *is*—to the ignoration of the actual!
    Sister Dora, the real sister of Mark Pattison :
what a comment on 'heredity and the non-existence
of a force of self-determining moral uprising !

It is objected—and mark, by the Positivist, to
whom by the necessity of his position the moral is an
impossibility—that the doctrine of the forgiveness of
sins is opposed to morality. Is it so ?
    Objectively viewed, the forgiveness of sins rests on

the basis of the possibility of moral restoration. Its fundamental idea is the capability of moral restoration. It is, or implies, what the old divines used to call *restitutio ad integrum*.

This *in limine* overthrows the Positivist objections. But further, subjectively viewed [of course I am discarding the washerwoman-theology about forgiveness] forgiveness implies : the consciousness of moral discord, and the desire for its removal. The idea of punishment is only an accident and concomitant, not the substance. Conscience speaks irrespective of all such sequents. Now we ofttimes in our loose thinking confound conscience with its application, i.e. its *dicta*. The *dicta* of conscience vary, one period or one nation may declare that wrong which to another had seemed right or at least indifferent. But while the *dicta* of conscience vary, conscience itself—that is, the acknowledgment of the absolute supremacy of a right, whatever that right may be—never varies. Consciences are varying in their mood ; conscience is permanent in its essence. And this acknowledgment of an absolute objective supremacy of right, does it not point to a Divine Law, and this Divine Law, in turn, to a Divine Revelation?

Assuredly, conscience in the sense of consciousness

of the absolute supremacy of *a* right, cannot be historically the offspring of fear.

To what has been said about the moral element as being the main idea underlying the doctrine of forgiveness, the same has to be added in regard to faith, as the Christian means for the reception of forgiveness.

Faith [though not in the mental or moral washer-woman-theology] is the highest moral effort: it is the victory of absolute moral objective truth over the empiricism of individual moral sentiment. Faith is not the crediting of certain historical statements, it is trust in God on the ground of these statements, the historical being the basis of the moral element in faith. *Christianity being an historical religion, its moral outcome is also based on historical facts*—trust on belief. But faith is trust (' with the heart man believeth unto righteousness '), and trust is in itself a moral attainment and victory over the presently seen. It is trust in God, notwithstanding the seen and felt of conscience—' God is greater than our hearts.' Trust is the element of contest and of victory in our upwards-striving; in fact, it necessarily leads to such upwards-striving. Trust gives glory to God; it does not ignore, rather presupposes, conscience; but it reaches to the

higher—God. Such faith is theologically and ethi-
cally the beginning and the principle of a new life.
Most truly do we by faith become alike objectively
and subjectively the children of God : the Divine is im-
ported into us, and we become Divine אַשְׁרֵי כָּל־חוֹסֵי בוֹ.

It has been objected that such outward results of
Christianity as almshouses, hospitals &c. are no good
at all, since the recipients of such charity had better
perish—better, that is, for humanity.

This, in the first place, ignores the moral good as
regards the bestower of charity.

It ignores, secondly, the absolute dignity of
humanity and consequent sanctity of life [which to
us Christians has become fully apparent by the
Incarnation].

But, if the reasoning of our objectors be valid,
can you stop midway at the *poor* diseased and inca-
pables ? Nay more—why stop at them ? Why suffer
many others who are far greater drones and nuisances
to remain ?

And as your rule as to what should remain or
be swept away is necessarily subjective, its results
would be an internecine war, the last survivor in
which should commit suicide. Such is logically your
ultimate goal. Positivism creates an earthly Pande-

monium which ends in desolation ; Christianity looks for a new earth and a new heaven wherein dwelleth righteousness.

Utilitarianism !   No ! the world is not a Mutual-Convenience Assurance Company, nor life to be the universal attainment of good social digestion and cure of all social dyspepsia.

All men are under some influence.   The question only is : *what* that influence is.

Men are mostly weaker, women mostly stronger, than we imagine.   A man is strongest in his 'hobby;' a woman weakest [every woman absolutely weak] in her love-affairs.

Much as one dreads setting up canons of criticism, a few such suggest themselves as the result of reason and experience.

1. The genuineness or spuriousness of a passage or a narrative must not be determined on subjective, but on objective grounds.   Its spuriousness must appear from the document itself, or else from the thing itself.   It is not sufficient to say that it seems

to me unlikely. In short, the criticism must be historical, not subjective.

2. Similarly, all tendency-criticism must be set aside. At present it is open to three objections: (a) you suppose the existence of a motive; (β) you suppose an individual to be open to that motive; (γ) you suppose that he was actually influenced by it. But even if your first two positions were established—and this can only be on historical grounds, not on surmises—your third inference would still be most unwarranted in the absence of historical evidence. If all who have some motive for stealing were, for example, to be regarded as thieves, there would be few persons out of prison.

Once more, then, I plead for historical as against subjective criticism.

3. Experience has taught me that there are many passages which bear marks of later ' editing '—in the form of additions or emendations—some perhaps originally added from the margin.

But there is not any evidence of an absolute invention of a whole book or narrative—nor do I believe such to have occurred.

Additions and emendations — glosses — are in character with this literature, but certainly not absolute falsehood.

4. All *suggestio mali* is to be eliminated, as being once more subjective criticism.   Similarly, all *a priori* reasoning is subjective, and unfitted for historical criticism.

5. All explanations which imply what is extremely artificial or exceedingly complicated, are self-condemned, such as many of those in regard to the composition of the Pentateuch.   They savour of the ingenuity of the German Professoriate, not of the simplicity and want of artificial training of the original writers.   You must find a simple theory if it is to deserve even serious examination.

6. Every critical question must be considered in connection with the circumstances, the culture, and the general conditions of the times.

After all, these six canons only mean the need of a strictly historical School of Criticism, as against the present *a priori*, subjective and theoretical criticism.

In viewing conscience as the felt supremacy of right, the need of Revelation seems implied, for otherwise our notions of what that right is would be subjective, and therefore varying ; or else only utilitarian, which is but another aspect of the subjective.

Therefore, if I believe that God is the Guide of all

good, and that He would guide man to good, there is implied in this a necessity of revelation. .

If I were to argue with a Jew, I would not allow him to discuss *a priori* the possibility of the miraculous Birth and Resurrection of the Christ, for miracles are the postulates of his religion, if it be that of the Old Testament. The only question between us can be that of their historical occurrence.

I do not object to the descent of people : only to the dirt which they bring down with it.

Some people always oscillate between faith and unbelief, like the pendulum of a Dutch clock, and with the same loud and disagreeable tick.

Many of our virtues are only the polished side of the blackened leather.

Every man has his own idol, unless he has a God.

How much are the opinions of men concerning us worth ? As much as you require to and can purchase with them. Yet, even if we do not require to purchase anything, unfortunately ready coin is required to pay the tolls along the road by which we are travelling.

Faith in God makes us optimists : experience of the world and of men, pessimists.

Can we be both at the same time ? Yes, by renouncing the world.

As regards the difficulty about the miracles, I wonder that those who believe in a personal God do not realise that the greatest of all miracles is a Personal God.

There was a distinct use in controversies in the Early Apostolic Church. At first, when there was no controversy, no question which elicited different answers in the bosom of the Christian Church, the teaching could only be parenetic. Thus the Epistle of St. James—according to Bürger (in Strack and Zöckler's *Commentary*), the earliest Christian writing, dating from between the death of James the Elder and the Apostolic Council (Acts xv.), before the time of St. Paul, and reflecting the period of ' undeveloped simple faith in Jesus as the Christ '—is simply practical [not doctrinal, still less anti-Pauline], and directed against the peculiar Jewish national failings and temptations [the Epistle is addressed to Jewish believers, in and out of Palestine].

Thus, the development of Christian doctrine was really due to controversy—rather, it was the answer of God to the questioning of the Church. Starting in the ignorance [or rather, non-knowledge] of a simple faith, the Church developed by the combined influence of new circumstances which arose in the course of her progress, and new questions which were raised in connection with it.

The Day of Pentecost is to the Church what Christmas was to the world. Then the Incarnate Christ came and dwelt on earth; at Pentecost the Holy Spirit became a real Personality to the Church [just as the Messiah became no longer a promise or prophetic anticipation]. He became as it were Incarnate, by taking up His permanent abode in the Church and in the soul of each believer.

The Day of Pentecost was God's morning greeting to the Church.

In St. Paul's writings, dogmatics and practical religion absolutely coincide. Each is also the other. A lesson, this, to us.

I find it more difficult to arrange my thoughts than to think. I suspect mine is the defect of the Eastern mind: to think in the succession of time—one thought suggesting the other, rather than in the succession of nature—one thought springing out of the other. In short, I am prone to think in intercalated sentences; and I like it.

The origin of the Diaconate is instructive as regards ecclesiastical institutions. It was not part of a preconceived system, nor even in any way premeditated, but due to a present necessity and felt want of the Church. I have even doubt whether it was at first intended to be a general institution. But circumstances and events similar to those which led to its first introduction at Jerusalem would soon lead to the institution of the Diaconate in other Churches, and gradually to its permanent order as one of the institutions in regularly organised Churches. But I do not think that with its expansion it retained its original character as alms-distributing—if indeed that was

ever more than a function, not the sum-total of the
office. And for the alms-distribution there was an
analogue in the Synagogue, though I do not believe
the Diaconate was even in Jerusalem simply an imi-
tation of it.

Mrs. Humphry Ward accuses me (in the 'Nineteenth
Century,' March 1889) of 'bad history' in my 'Jesus
the Messiah.' It is difficult to refute a general accusa-
tion unsupported by specific evidence. By the modern
method of history is often meant the method of
reading modern ideas into ancient history. But
in the present instance Mrs. Ward only shows her
ignorance of the whole scope of my book, to which
her hero is supposed to have given 'some hours'
of study. My object—which was carried out in the
examination of every Gospel narrative—was to trans-
port myself into those times, and to show that the
life and teaching of Jesus—His conception of the
Kingdom of God and of the Messiahship—were absolutely opposed to the ideas and conceptions of His
time and people: that the ideal which He realised
was the contrary of that for the embodiment of
which they looked. Or, to put it otherwise: the
incidents of His life recorded in the Gospels, are the
opposite of those which His contemporaries would

K

have expected in the history of their Messiah ; and a
' Life ' written from the contemporary point of expectation would *not* have contained such incidents,
but presented a picture absolutely different from that
in the Gospels.   And this explains the opposition
unto death of the leaders of the Synagogue.

We are reproached that we treat not the historical
documents of the Bible in exactly the same manner as
the ordinary history of those times in which the
miraculous and the legendary were accepted.   Now
there are here two points of view. . . .[1]

[The two following fragments, found amongst Dr.
Edersheim's papers, are here inserted as perhaps being
of some general interest.]

1. *A New Translation of the Vision, Isaiah VI.*

EVEN within the compass of the Prophecies of Isaiah,
there is no portion more sublime in its imagery, or
solemn in its utterances, than the grand vision
recorded in the sixth chapter.   It is, so to speak, an
Old Testament anticipation of the Book of Revelation.

---

[1] This sentence was left unfinished.

The holy seer seems to stand within the great Palace of heaven. He beholds that majesty and glory at sight of which St. John 'fell at His feet as dead' (Rev. i. 17); he hears voices like those which filled the Beloved Disciple with such awe (Rev. iv. 5); and he receives in brief outline a prophetic message similar to that which the holy Apostle was directed to write out in detail for the instruction of the Church (Rev. i. 19). Only in the prophecies of Isaiah we are on strictly Old Testament ground, though with widest application to all men, since the proclamation is of 'Jehovah of Hosts,' whose 'glory fills the whole earth.'

Yet most truly is it of the Old Testament, alike in the prophet's sense of personal sinfulness, in the symbolic cleansing of his lips, and in the message which he is directed to deliver specially to God's ancient people Israel. Without entering on a detailed examination of what might otherwise be of deepest interest, two general remarks may here be allowed. *First*: The *date* of this prophecy—'in the death-year of King Uzziah'—is of deepest significance. We remember that, as St. Jerome remarked, this date synchronizes with the year of the foundation of Imperial Rome (about 754 B.C.). In that year, then, most significantly, did the death-knell of Israel's glory first strike in the Palace of the Great King. *Secondly*:

We mark the proclamation of Jehovah into all the
world as 'The Holy One.' This designation of God
is as characteristic of the prophecies of Isaiah as that
' My Father' was in the utterances of Jesus. Only
in the prophecies of Isaiah He is—in accordance with
the Old Dispensation—chiefly presented as ' The Holy
One of Israel.' A learned Italian Rabbi, Luzzatto,
has noted it as characteristic of the prophecies of
Isaiah, that they all have this designation of God as
their peculiar mark—*we* should say, like the personal
salutation-signature of St. Paul as the token in every
epistle, so he wrote (2 Thess. iii. 17). Similarly, we
recognise the unity of the prophecies of Isaiah by this
their headmark, or what Luzzatto calls ' the device
graven on the signet-ring.' The designation ' Holy
One of Israel,' which occurs only three times in the
Psalms (lxxi. 22 ; lxxviii. 41 ; lxxxix. 19) ; and twice
in the prophecies of Jeremiah—and, as *Delitzsch*
suggests, probably with reference to Isaiah (Jer. l. 29 ;
li. 5)—is found no less than twenty-nine times in the
prophecies of Isaiah : twelve times in the first part
(chs. i.–xxxix.), and seventeen times in the second
part (chs. xl.–lxvi.). Thus the inscription : ' The
Holy One of Israel '—the subject of the Trishagion of
the love-' burning ' seraphs, the grand new revelation
to Isaiah, presently to be the burden of his message—

is like the keystone which binds together the arch of these prophecies.

But, as already stated, it is not the object of this brief paper to examine in detail the vision of Isaiah vi. Our present purpose rather is to rectify a misinterpretation of the last verse of this prophecy, which seems to render its understanding well-nigh impossible. Perhaps, however, it may be well to preface it with a fresh rendering of the whole prophecy. As here rendered, it seems to fall into four stanzas—the first of four, the others of three verses each:

1. In the death-year of the King Uzziah:
 I saw the Lord sitting upon a throne high and uplifted,
  And His skirts filling the Palace—
2. Seraphim standing from over it—six wings, six wings to each,
 With two he is covering his face, and with two covering his feet, and on two he is winging,
3. And cries this one to that, and says: Holy, Holy, Holy, Jehovah of Hosts,
  Filling all the earth His glory!
4. And trembled foundations (mothers) of the thresholds from the voice of the crying (one),[1]
 And the house became filled with smoke.

---

[1] The 'crying one' here corresponds to the 'Coming One' as the designation of the Messiah (St. Mark i. 7). Thus, the vision is like a John the Baptist's announcement, only this time in the Palace of heaven, not in the wilderness of earth.

5. And I said : Woe me, for I, a man unclean of lips, and
    in the midst of a people unclean of lips dwelling,
  Because the King[1] Jehovah of Hosts have seen my eyes.
6. And winged to me one from the Seraphim, and in his
    hand a glowing coal,
  With tongs took he (it) from off the altar—
7. And he touched upon my mouth, and said : Behold,
    touched this on thy lips—
  And removed has thy transgression, and thy sin has
    been atoned ![2]

8. And I heard the voice of the Lord saying : Whom shall
    I send ? And who will go for us ?
      And I said, Behold, I—send me.
9. And He said : Go and speak to this people :
  Hear ye hearing, and ye will not understand ; and see
    ye seeing, and ye will not know.
10. Make fat the heart of this people, and their ears make
    heavy, and their eyes daub over,
  Lest they should see with their eyes, and with their ears
    hear, and their heart understand, and it return, and
    He give it healing.

11.   And I said : To how long, O Lord ?—
  And He said : To this—When desolated are cities, with-
    out dweller, and houses, without human being,
  And the land shall have been laid waste, a desolateness,

---

[1] In the Hebrew : אֶת־הַמֶּלֶךְ The Rabbis hold it as a hermeneutic
canon, that the אֵת, which is really a note of the accusative, indicates
that the word before which it stands is *inclusive* in its meaning—
marks this and something else along with it. The אֵת occurs again
in ver. 8 : '*Whom* shall I send ? '
[2] ' Covered,' as in the Atonement.

12.   And far removed has Jehovah man,
And great the desolateness within the land—
13. And yet therein a tenth, and it shall return, and (though)
   it be for burning—
   (Yet) like the terebinth and like the oak which, in the
   felling, a stock in them :
   Holy seed the stock !

The last verse, which really contains the gist of the
prophecy, so far as its promise to Israel is concerned,
will, it is hoped, become intelligible in the version
above proposed. Our English Bible renders verse 13 :
'But yet in it shall be a tenth, and it shall return,
and shall be eaten : as a teil tree, and as an oak,
whose substance is in them, when they cast their
leaves : so the holy seed shall be the substance thereof.'
The reader would find it difficult to understand the
meaning of these words, even as emendated in the
margin. Dr. Kay in the 'Speaker's Commentary' proposes to translate, 'But there is still in it a tenth, and
it shall return, and shall be for burning : as a terebinth,
and as an oak which on shedding its leaves hath its
substance in it, so the holy seed shall be the substance
thereof.' But there is twofold objection to this translation. 1stly, the rendering 'shedding its leaves,'
although suggested by Rabbinic authority, is so forced
in the meaning which it assigns to the Hebrew, as

to be inadmissible.   2ndly : It is impossible to see
the connection between the illustrative clause with
which the vision closes.   It is difficult to understand
how, if not only Israel, but its remnant, 'the tenth,'
presumably 'the holy seed,' is 'for burning,' the
illustration of the terebinth and oak 'which on shedding
its leaves hath its substance in it,' is at all applicable.

A similar objection applies to the rendering of
Professor Delitzsch, which, as adopted by Mr. Cheyne
in his recently published learned Commentary on
Isaiah, may here find a place.   Both critics translate :
'And should there yet be a tenth in it, this shall
again be exterminated, as the terebinth and as the
oak, of which, after the felling, a stock remaineth,
a holy seed is the stock thereof.'   To this rendering
there are 1stly : certain linguistic objections.   To
waive minor difficulties, the words (italicised) : 'And
should there yet *be* a tenth in it,' are not in the text,
but a gloss of the interpreter.   Again, in the next
clause, the word '*again*' is so forced a rendering as to
be almost impossible, while what is rendered 'exterminated' bears this only as its secondary meaning, the
primary being 'to burn.'   But 2ndly : the rendering of Professors Delitzsch and Cheyne entirely
destroys the meaning of the illustrative clause, on

which evidently the whole turns. If 'the tenth,' presumably 'the holy seed,' shall again be 'exterminated,' how is the remnant-stock of the oak as, after the trunk is cut down, it sprouts forth afresh, to be an illustration thereof—or what in such case is the meaning of the illustration ?

All these difficulties are, we submit, removed by our proposed translation. No objection can be urged against it on linguistic grounds, since it is strictly literal. And the meaning of the illustration becomes now perfectly clear. Israel as a nation is like the terebinth or the oak which has been felled in judgment. But yet there is a holy remnant, as it were the LORD's tithe, consecrated to Him. It shall return, and though it—whether the wood of the felled oak or even the small remnant (more probably, the former)—'be for burning,' yet this 'holy seed' is the still living 'stock' which, when the tree has been felled, sprouts forth afresh in new life.

Thus viewed, this prophecy also is not only of Israel, but of Christ—or rather of His Kingdom. And it stands aptly at the head of all the prophecies of Isaiah. For, in truth, they are but the unfolding of what this first vision infolds.

2. *Scheme of possible Lectures on* The Problems of
the Faith.

1. The Book of Genesis.

2. The Incarnation and Resurrection of Christ.

3. Jesus of Nazareth the great historical Problem.

4. The Book of Ecclesiastes.

5. What Christ makes clear to us : God, our
eternal life—man, and his brotherhood—the highest
moral ideal, the kingdom : whence all this if not of
God ?

6. Christianity historically considered — in its
effects and result.

7. The inward structure of the Bible—two sets
of facts : material, or of outward experience, and
spiritual, or of inward experience. The solution is
not the elimination of the one or the other, but their
inward conciliation.

8. The development of teaching in the Bible, and
its progressive advancement.

9. The personification of the Divine in the Old
Testament (common in the East to devout minds, and
with a deep background of truth) as explaining some
difficulties, such as the wars of extermination, the
vengeance-Psalms &c.

10. On the limits of our religious knowledge and
religious certitude.

11. On the ideal Church of the future.

12. On Christianity as the faith in the Christ—the hope of the Christ—and the love to the Christ : glory to God in the highest, peace on earth, and goodwill towards men.

13. On the *Chochmah*-literature of the Old Testament and the Apocrypha. The place of the *Torah* is occupied by *Chochmah* : very characteristic here is a comparison of Ps. i. 2, ובתורתו יהנה with Ecclus. xiv. 20, ὃς ἐν σοφίᾳ μελετήσει. Soon after the return from the Exile, Grecianism passed as a wave over Palestine. To this we owe the *Chochmah*-literature in its present form, which sought its sanction and traced up its tending to Solomon, as the wise king. This evoked the reaction of orthodoxy, in which the *Chasidim* appeared, appealing as the word shows to David. Under this influence Pharisaism is developed, while Grecianism passed into the Diaspora to be there finally developed. But this also reflects on the age of the Pentateuch—especially of the *Priest-Code*. Evidently that was in the remote distance, and no one of the Grecians thought of ascribing this—to them hostile—element to the spurious introduction by the priests at a comparatively quite recent period. It is a mistake to suppose that Grecianism originated merely in the *Zeitgeist*. It had struck its

roots in the *Chochmah* writings of Palestine, and only took occasion from, and developed under, the fostering influence as Alexandrianism.

[The following table talk is from some notes of his conversation, made by one of Dr. Edersheim's daughters during the early weeks of 1882.]

Speaking of two rogues, the one strong and healthy in body, the other weakly, he said : ' Mistrust the latter the most, the mind being likely to be the most developed.'

Speaking of Carlyle—how much he is abused now-a-days—he said : ' A great personality casts a great shadow.   People now have forgotten the personality, and look only at the shadow.'

When there was some talk of the possible immorality of proverbs, he said : ' Proverbs are the devil's markers when he plays at cards.'

We all gave our ideas of happiness.   His was : ' a *palazzo* in a good climate, with enough money to do nothing but study and write at leisure.'

We were wondering what would become of Zing's good qualities after his death. [Zing was his favourite white Pomeranian dog.]   He said it was the great mystery of nature.   He added that, as nature abhors a vacuum, so self-consciousness abhors extinction.

We were urging him to write his life: it would be so interesting.   He said, 'No.   I have played the dancing-bear long enough in my life before the eyes of people, to wish to do it when I am dead.'

'When people have literally nothing to do, they must take to cards, drink, or gossip.'

'There is no ignorance so dangerous as experienced ignorance.'

'I think that in religion there should be the utmost liberty, to Mahomedan, Hindoo, all, alike.'

On one occasion he asked this daughter why she was so silent.   She made answer: 'Because I have nothing to say;' to which he replied: 'People generally talk most then.'

[The accompanying hymns are selected from a number translated from the German during a period of illness and enforced idleness in the winter of 1870–71. The first three were adapted to airs from Mendelssohn's *Lieder ohne Worte*; the last, from the German of Ernst von Feuchtersleben (*circa* 1826), had already been set to music by Mendelssohn in 1839.]

I

I'll take what Thou art pleased to send,
And yield if Thou no longer lend;
I'll come if Thou the way wilt show,
And flee where Thou forbid'st to go.

Come joy or grief, content I'll rest
And feel myself supremely blest,
Since nought in earth or heaven can part
The Saviour from the loving heart.

So then I'll choose not what I will,
But calmly rest in Thee, be still,
And, guided by Thy gracious Hand,
With Thee begin and with Thee end.

Yet pity Thou my weakness, Lord,
And speak again the plighted word:
That nought can e'er betide to part
From Thee my weak and fainting heart.

II

Oh, turn again, oh, turn again,
Bring all thy sorrow, all thy pain,
Return thou weary one at last,
And at His feet thy burden cast!
No need to wait for change of heart,
The welcome meets thee as thou art!
Behold, the Father's loving Face
Is bent on thee; His word of grace
It speaks to thee : ' Come, welcome thou! '
Oh, turn again, nor linger now!

Oh, turn again! Life from above
Lies in the fulness of His love;
The Lord is patient, beareth long,
Abundantly forgives the wrong.
Then from His heart of love take heart :
He has a balm for every smart,
And gives most sure and sweet relief
In every sickness, every grief—
Oh, stay no longer to be blest :
Return to Him, and in Him rest!

Oh, turn again, return at last
Unto thy home, thy wanderings past—
From death to everlasting life,
To heavenly peace from burning strife,
From the false to truth abiding,
And from want to rich providing;
To the real from the seeming,
And from darkness to the gleaming;
But what the Lord would give to-day,
Take now—and turn without delay!

III

The Lord He knows His chosen band,
  And ever knew them all,
In every age and every land,
  Alike the great and small.

Our faithful Shepherd will His sheep
  In tender mercy bear;
In life and death He'll safely keep
  The objects of His care.

What marks each one within the fold
  Is faith which does not see,
And yet, as if it did behold,
  Trusts, unseen Lord, to Thee.

Let us, who now Thy throne surround,
  With plea of Jesu's Name,
Each share that faith, in it abound,
  And keep us in the same.

To that within the veil let fast
  Our hope, as anchor, cling:
In life of love, all old things past,
  Let love its homage bring.

And, when that glorious day shall shine,
  The world its King shall see:
Then own us, blessed Lord, as Thine,
  And call us up to Thee !

IV

It is the Lord of Heaven's behest,
That each from what he loves the best
Must parted be!
Though nought in course of earthly things
Such grief and sorrow ever brings
As such farewell—
Ah me, farewell!

If here some opening bud thou find,
Oh, tend it with a loving mind:
But be thou ware!
The rose that bursts at morn in bloom,
Lies withered in the midnight gloom—
Of this be ware,
Ah, be thou ware!

The love thou fondly callest thine,
With watchful, miser care enshrine
Within thy heart!
A little while thy joy is left—
And then, thou art again bereft,
To weep alone,
Ah, weep alone!

Yet, see thou understand it right:
Yes, know aright!
When here we part, each in his way,
' To meet again!' we fondly say,
To meet again!
Yes, meet again!

L

INDEX OF SUBJECTS

Spottiswoode & Co., Printers, New-street Square, London.

CPSIA information can be obtained
at www.ICGtesting.com
Printed in the USA
LVHW052202221218
601333LV00008B/304/P